DARK GOD

CRUELTY, SEX, AND VIOLENCE IN THE OLD TESTAMENT

THOMAS RÖMER

GW00673440

Paulist Press
New York / Mahwah, NJ

Cover image by jorisvo/Shutterstock.com
Cover and book design by Lynn Else
Text illustrations courtesy of Prof. Othmar Keel (Fribourg). Used with permission. All rights reserved.

Originally published as: *Dieu obscur. Cruauté, sexe et violence dans l'Ancien Testament. Series: Essais bibliques*, copyright © 2009 by Editions Labor et Fides, Genève, Switzerland.
Third edition
English translation by Sean O'Neill

Library of Congress Cataloging-in-Publication Data

Römer, Thomas, 1955-
    [Dieu obscur. English]
    Dark God : cruelty, sex, and violence in the Old Testament / Thomas Römer.
        pages cm
    Includes bibliographical references (pages   ).
    ISBN 978-0-8091-4796-0 (alk. paper)
    1. Bible. O.T.—Theology. 2. Hidden God. I. Title.
    BS1192.6.R6513 2013
    231—dc23

                                                              2012042484

ISBN: 978-0-8091-4796-0 (paperback)

Published by Paulist Press
997 Macarthur Boulevard
Mahwah, New Jersey 07430

www.paulistpress.com

Printed and bound in the
United States of America

CONTENTS

PREFACE

This is the third edition of a book that was written to address directly some of the questions that the public often raises concerning the God of the Old Testament. In several texts from the Hebrew Bible, particularly in episodes where God appears far from politically correct, the image of God runs contrary to our common understanding of justice, nonviolence, or equality. How can we understand and speak of these issues without choosing selective or apologetic interpretations of the Bible, or without reducing some of these characteristics to outdated forms of religion that were valid only for believers of another age? This book presents answers that lead the reader to rediscover some of these "difficult" passages and texts and provides historical analysis, comparison, and interpretation to shed light on some little-understood aspects that are nevertheless worthwhile. This version of the book builds on the second edition, but has been completely revised and here and there rounded off, notably by the addition of a new chapter: "Is God Self-Righteous and Humans Mere Sinners?"

Unfortunately, the observation made in the preface to the first edition still holds true:

> At a time when fundamentalist religious ideas, whether they rely on the Bible or the Koran, are becoming more alarmingly widespread, it is impossible to ignore texts that present God as violating human rights or perpetrating ethnic

cleansing. I have tried to show that the Old Testament texts that might shock us have arisen in specific historical circumstances and that it is theologically inadmissible to use these texts indiscriminately, whatever the reason.

I have dedicated this work to my two teachers who have inspired and stimulated my interest in the Old Testament and helped me to avoid an overly "orthodox" interpretation of the Hebrew Bible: Rolf Rendtorff, who was my professor at Heidelberg, and Françoise Smyth-Florentin in Paris, who opened to me the world of French commentary on biblical texts.

Of course, this small book is in no way an exhaustive treatise on what the Old Testament has to say about God and humanity. Its aim is simply to provide help in discerning in our founding Scriptures those elements that give rise to the worst historical misunderstandings. This in turn provides room in which we may exercise our judgment as believers or nonbelievers.

Finally, I would particularly like to thank Labor et Fides Editions and especially Ms. Muriel Füllemann and M. Gabriel de Montmollin for the invaluable help they brought to the new edition of this book.

Thomas Römer
Lausanne and Paris, September 2009

The translations of the biblical texts are taken from the NRSV and occasionally are slightly modified. The illustrations come from various books by Professor Othmar Keel (Fribourg), and are used with his kind permission.

THE CHALLENGE OF THE OLD TESTAMENT GOD

References to the God of the Old Testament can elicit a whole set of negative images among laypeople: notably that of a God who is primitive, angry, jealous, and unpredictable. Feminists would undoubtedly add *sexist* to that list. This "politically incorrect" God seems opposed to the apparent love, compassion, and forgiveness of the New Testament God.

A brief overview of the Old Testament seems, at first glance, to back up this impression. Right from the first book of the Bible, we see God the Creator putting in place a restriction on eating from a certain tree, a restriction that will inevitably be violated by the first human couple and that will lead all of humanity into a cycle of rebellion and ruthless reprisals (Gen 2:17). The man and his wife are thrown out of the garden, but that punishment is nothing compared to what God does, a few chapters later, when he drowns the entire human race, sparing only Noah and his family. Once humanity has been established again, God apparently cannot tolerate man's ambition and technical progress: the city and tower of Babel are ruined, and humanity is dispersed to the four corners of the earth.

The narrative of the patriarchs seems to begin more promisingly, in that God shows great concern for Abraham.

But the patriarch Abraham also comes to experience God as hard and incomprehensible, principally because God demands that he sacrifice his beloved son Isaac. In addition, God himself seems to have the characteristics of a patriarch, tolerating all sorts of scheming and dishonest behavior, notably on the part of Jacob, the ancestor of his future people.

On the other hand, the Exodus story that follows is one of liberation, in which God takes the side of the oppressed, delivering them from the hands of tyrants. This is true, and yet in the same book we again encounter a God of anger—for example, in the killing of the firstborn of the Egyptians on the night before the exodus from Egypt, or in the ruthless suppression of the Israelites who had indulged in the cult of the golden calf. Even before these events, God expresses his desire, for reasons that remain unknown to us, to kill Moses, whom he had called to his service.

Finally, the Law itself is not short on instructions that seem to us today to be characterized by cruelty. Thus, Deuteronomy 13 describes the extermination of an entire city because the inhabitants became interested in gods other than the God of Israel. It is no wonder, then, that the God of the Old Testament comes across as an avenger. This image is consistent with what we find in the Prophets, notably Amos and Micah, who appear to do nothing but preach the anger of God and announce his judgment over Israel. We can also find this severe view of history within the great historiographical work that starts with Deuteronomy and ends with 2 Kings, which presents the destruction of Jerusalem by the Babylonians in 587 BC as a judgment willed by God.

This atmosphere, marked by God's intransigence and anger, is received particularly badly by people today since it is expressed through the language of jealousy, in which the victims are not only other gods, but also the people of

Israel, who risked being seduced by other rival gods. Similarly, in the biblical stories of conquest and the brutal extermination of enemies, the image of a warlike and totalitarian God persists and is closely associated with the God of the Old Testament.

Hostility toward the God of the Old Testament is not a modern phenomenon. In the history of emerging Christianity, the best-known example of this hostility is undoubtedly Marcion, who lived in the middle of the second century AD. This shipowner and theologian was strongly influenced by Gnosticism[1] and an interpretation of the Pauline Epistles that emphasized the opposition between the Law and the Gospel. For Marcion, the God of the Old Testament was a "demiurge," a minor god who was responsible for creating evil, who held to the principle of retribution, and who was devoid of goodness and love. With Christ, according to Marcion, there arose a new revelation founded on pure goodness, a quality that had remained unknown to material creation and its creator. Around AD 144, Marcion broke off from the Christian community of Rome and founded his own church, which became very powerful and which survived until the era of Constantine. According to his approach, Marcion rejected the whole of the Old Testament, maintaining that it was a witness to a cruel and bloodthirsty God. From the New Testament, he accepted only the Pauline Epistles and the Gospel of Luke, with revisions and corrections.

The hostile tendencies toward the God of the Old Testament, however, did not disappear at the same time as the Marcionite community. We do not have space here to trace the entire history of the rejection of the God of the Old Testament throughout the centuries. Instead, we will mention only that during the eras of Rationalism and of the

Enlightenment many Old Testament statements about God were considered primitive and opposed to enlightened morality. Around 1774, the theologian Johann Salomo Semler (1725–91) wrote: "As a general rule, Christians cannot come to a knowledge of God through the books of the Old Testament but only through the perfect doctrine of Christ and his apostles."[2] We can also find this opinion in Friedrich Schleiermacher (1768–1834). In his presentation of the Christian faith, the Old Testament is almost eliminated. It is the New Testament writings that constitute the norm of Christian doctrine, and it is the Spirit and not the letter of the Law that characterizes this doctrine. Schleiermacher even suggests presenting the Old Testament in Christian Bibles as an appendix, in order to show the discordance between the God of Israel and the God of Jesus Christ.

A century later, Christian reservations regarding the Old Testament are expressed by the great scholar Adolf von Harnack (1851–1930) in a book dedicated to Marcion. There he puts forward the oft-quoted suggestion: "Rejecting the Old Testament in the second century was an error that the Church rightly avoided. Keeping it in the sixteenth century was a fate that even the Reformation could not escape. But to preserve it in the nineteenth century as a canonical document at the heart of Protestantism is a result of religious and ecclesiastical paralysis."[3]

Unfortunately, it is not surprising that in the 1930s very influential German literature existed in which animosity against the God of Israel manifested itself in the service of the Nazi ideology. A notable example is *The False God: Evidence against Yahweh* (*Der falsche Gott. Beweismaterial gegen Jahwe*) by the anti-Semitic author Theodor Fritsch (1852–1933).[4]

At the same time, Emmanuel Hirsch (1888–1972), in what is a decidedly more theological perspective, uses the opposition between the Law and the Gospel to characterize the relationship between the God of the Old and the New Testaments by taking Lutheran theology on board wholesale. According to Hirsch, the Old Testament is entirely "materialistic." It ignores the dialectic of the two kingdoms and covers only God's earthly government. The God of Abraham in Genesis 22, for example, is different from the Father of Jesus Christ in the sense that he requires blind obedience to his orders. The God of the Old Testament appears as a disturbing and demanding power before whom human beings must bow down.[5]

This vision of the God of the Old Testament can also be found in some of the writings of the theologian and great New Testament scholar Rudolf Bultmann (1884–1976). For Bultmann, God's commandments make human beings aware of the consequences of living under the influence of the Law, and it is the Gospel that frees them from this subjection. The Old Testament thus becomes for Bultmann a kind of symbol describing the alienated relationship between God and mankind.[6]

Certainly, after the end of World War II, the image of the God of the Old Testament improves considerably among Christians, and notably in certain Protestant circles that felt close to Judaism. Here the pendulum swings the other way. All that might appear forbidding and incomprehensible in the Old Testament texts is either erased or is too quickly assimilated into apologetic and harmonious readings. More recently, however, the three monotheistic religions have been criticized in some publications for having prepared the way for totalitarianism. The basis of all these ills is once again the God of the Jewish Bible: "Believers' [that is, Abraham's] submission to the Father...calls for blind obedience to rules and opens the way to crimes against humanity."[7]

Given this situation, which is often characterized by overly psychological or even fanciful readings of the great religious texts of humanity, it is essential to confront the disturbing, scandalous, or ambiguous aspects of the "personality" of the God of the Old Testament.

REFUSING TO ACKNOWLEDGE HISTORICAL CONTEXT

The rejection by some contemporary scholars of certain Old Testament passages regarding God seems to me to be the result of an uncritical reading of the Hebrew Bible, a reading that fails to take into account the historical setting and cultural circumstances of the Old Testament itself. The God of the Old Testament has a history and it is important not to omit it. Today, if one were to edit an anthology of discourses on God by the Fathers of the Church, medieval scholastic figures, reformers, representatives of the Enlightenment, atheistic philosophers, and the greatest contemporary theologians, no one would read such a compilation in a way that did not take historical context into consideration, as if all those writings dated from the same era. Rather, readers would attempt to understand these various writings as products of specific periods and circumstances in which writers spoke about God in certain ways.

Similarly, in order to have serious theological reflection on the God of the Old Testament, it is important first to take into account the diversity of the various testimonies. How is it possible to speak of the same God in such a variety of different ways? The answer to a question of this kind necessarily becomes a historical investigation and requires a willingness to place oneself in the conceptual and ideological context of the authors of those testimonies. The God of the Old Testament was first worshipped in the Levant long before the writings of the Bible were fixed into the formal canon that we now use to understand God. Therefore, we must begin our approach by retracing briefly the different ways in which Israel accounted for its God. In other words, we must put forth a brief "biography" of the God that Judaism, Christianity, and Islam confess, respectively, as the God of Israel, the God of Jesus Christ, and the One God.

THE EVOLUTION OF IDEAS ABOUT THE GOD OF ISRAEL

The Old Testament can be read either as a collection of the holy scriptures of Judaism or as the first part of the Christian Bible. From this point of view, it bears witness to the one and only God who created the world, sustains it, and will lead it to its ultimate destination. Therefore, the Hebrew Bible is presented as a monotheistically based document. The summary of the Jewish faith that we find in Deuteronomy 6:4—"Hear, O Israel: The LORD is our God, the LORD alone"—is clearly understood as the most succinct expression of monotheism, even if this text originally had a different aim (which we will return to later). This monotheistic confession, which forms the basis of Judaism, Christianity, and Islam, does not reflect an unchanging idea that existed from the very beginning. No, the people of Israel came to this understanding of God gradually throughout the course of their long history.

Despite its resolutely monotheistic aim, there are several clues within the Old Testament that show us that for a number of centuries Yahweh, or Yaho—as the God of Israel was called, a name that many devout Jews will not utter[8]—was not the only god that was accepted and known in Israel.

First, let us consider the original version of the "Song of Moses" in Deuteronomy 32. In this version, which we can reconstruct from the Greek translation and from one of the Qumran[9] Hebrew manuscripts, we read in verse 8:

> When the Most High [El Elyon] apportioned the
>   nations,
>   when he divided humankind,
> he fixed the boundaries of the peoples
>   according to the number of the gods
>   [the sons of El];
> the LORD's [Yhwh's] own portion was his people,
>   Jacob his allotted share.

According to this version, the chief god, called El, divided the world according to the number of his sons, and Yhwh then receives the people of Israel as his possession. This text reflects the concept of a pantheon composed of different national gods under the aegis of a great god "El." The gods of the Israelites, the Moabites, the Edomites, and others, are considered to be brothers, having each received a people of which they are the lords and protectors.

YHWH, THE NATIONAL GOD OF THE MONARCHY

With the establishment of the monarchy, Yhwh went from being a tribal god to a national God. After Israel divided into northern and southern kingdoms around 926 BC, Yhwh was venerated as the national God in both Israel (the Northern Kingdom, also referred to as Samaria), and in

Judah (the Southern Kingdom). He was worshipped at open-air sanctuaries (called the "high places" in the Bible), and the worship of Yhwh was also celebrated in the royal sanctuaries: Jerusalem in the south; Bethel, Dan, and Samaria in the north.

What does the integration of the worship of Yhwh into the royal ideology mean? In order to understand that, it is necessary to realize first that the authority of a chief or king over a community or over a people was exercised in a comprehensive, rather than piecemeal, way. The whole of a community's life was determined by that authority. The king then was understood as the vicar of God who provides the link between the divine and human spheres. This mediation can be expressed in different ways:

1. The king himself is considered to be a god or is identified as a god.
2. The king bears the title "son of God," either because he had been directly begotten by a god or because he was adopted by a god upon his enthronement. This seems to be the current concept in Judah-Israel as shown by Psalm 2, which celebrates the accession of the king to the throne and where God says to the new king: "You are my son; / today I have begotten you" (v 7).
3. The king is also known as "the image of God," above all in Egypt. This term indicates the close relationship between the deity and the king: there is no other way to God except through his image, the king.

Through the king, the national god functions as a guarantee of health and well-being, promoting the fertility of the soil and an abundance of cattle. He is the supreme judge ensuring balance within the community. The national god is expected to protect and help, especially in the event of war. The "official" veneration of Yhwh during the royal era is hardly any different from the veneration of national gods among Israel's and Judah's neighbors. It is also clear that Yhwh was not the only divine being who was worshipped by the people of Israel. In this regard, the criticism of the prophets is significant. In Jeremiah 2:28, we read: "You have as many gods as you have towns, O Judah." Similarly, the iconographic evidence of the ninth to sixth centuries BC in Israel and Judah bear witness to the representation of numerous deities. The official religion of Israel's monarchy, therefore, was a *polytheistic* religion.

It is worthwhile here to mention a few words on polytheism. Scholars long considered polytheism a form of religious thought that indicated a primitive mental state, or, conversely, that represented a degeneration of an original monotheism. In fact, polytheism in its more elaborate forms only appears in civilizations that have achieved a high degree of complexity, either through having a political hierarchy or by differentiating the organization of work. The complex world of mankind, then, is reflected in the celestial realm where the same variety of domains is represented. The world of the gods is carried over into the world of humans and serves to guarantee its existence and structure. Thus, we find in the Old Testament several texts, particularly in the psalms, but also in the prologue to the Book of Job, where the God of Israel appears as a king surrounded by his court, as is the case with a human king. In legitimizing the existing social order, polytheism displays a very conservative tendency. The affirmation of a monotheistic faith, on the other hand, seems to be always linked to a dissenting movement, which attacks not only polytheistic religion, but also the political structures associated with it.

The Origins of the Worship of Yhwh Alone

What historical contexts in the Bible favored the worship of Yhwh alone and the rejection of the worship of any other gods? The biblical texts themselves place the fight for the sole worship of Yhwh in the general context of the struggle against Baal. Who is Baal? First, we must remember that the word *baal* was not originally a proper name. It is a form of address that is widespread in a number of Semitic languages and that means "master," "husband," or "lord." This title is principally applied to the god of tempest and fertility named Hadad in Syria or Melqart in Tyre. By studying the Old Testament, we make a disturbing discovery: in some texts Yhwh is depicted with very Baal-like traits. For example, he bears the epithet "rider on the clouds" (Ps 68:34; Deut 33:26), which the texts from Ugarit frequently use in reference to Baal. (Ugarit was an ancient Canaanite port city near Ras Shamra—Lattakia in modern Syria—where texts on clay tablets were discovered that reflect Canaanite religion at the end of the second millennium BC.) Like Baal of the Canaanites, Yhwh dwells on a mountain and, like Baal, he gives rain, fertility, and the harvest.

So where does this fierce battle against Baal in the Old Testament come from? One decisive moment occurred in the ninth century in the Northern Kingdom. It seems that Ahab, king of the dynasty of the Omrides, who was married to Jezebel, a Phoenician princess, had attempted to make the Phoenician god Melqart the protecting deity of the dynasty of the Omrides (cf. 1 Kgs 16:32; 2 Kgs 10:18–27). This god rightly bears the epithet "Baal of Tyre." It is in this context that we must understand both the conflict between the prophet Elijah and Ahab the king, and the bloody revolution of Jehu that overthrew the established dynasty. These events, principally in the prophetic context, reveal that there were other Baals besides Yhwh, gods who performed the same functions as Yhwh and who would have been in competition with him. This would lead some prophetic circles, which were initially very marginal, to reject the royal concept of a national god surrounded by other deities. This radical, exclusivist Yahwist movement perhaps had its origins in a tribal conception, probably dating back to the premonarchic era. However, we cannot go into this in much detail here.[10]

In the Old Testament, the first representative of this movement, which some exegetes have called "the Yhwh-alone party," was perhaps the prophet Hosea. For him, the Assyrian Empire that threatened the Northern Kingdom of Israel represented both the coming divine judgment and Israel's obligation to refrain from religious practices that were common in the Middle East: a diversity of gods, the statues and symbols of gods in the sanctuaries, soothsaying, and so on. Hosea also uses the image of a couple to illustrate his accusations: Israel, the spouse, has become unfaithful to Yhwh, her husband (that is, her "baal"). This view remained of minor significance in the North. However, when the Northern Kingdom fell to Assyria in 722, this "Yhwh-alone" message resonated loudly. In effect, the transformation of the North into a province of Assyria was the first time the idea of a national god was questioned. According to Assyrian practices, the God of Israel was symbolically declared a vassal of the national god of the Assyrians. The Assyrians, in fact, destroyed or deported the statues of the gods of the countries they vanquished to Assyria, set them up for a time in the Assyrian temples, and then returned them. Doing this was meant to signify the fact that the gods of conquered peoples had made an act of submission to, and an allegiance with, the Assyrian god.

How did the Southern Kingdom, that is, the Kingdom of Judah, react to the fall of the Northern Kingdom (Samaria) to the Assyrians? Apparently, the royal polytheistic cult was not undermined at first, and the South could declare itself the "true" people of Yhwh. It could be that the people of the Kingdom of Judah were rather content to see the disappearance of their brother enemies and the rival Yhwh of Samaria. Wasn't this proof positive that the "true" Yhwh was in Judah? Moreover, when the siege of Jerusalem, undertaken by the Assyrians in 701, was suddenly abandoned for reasons that remain obscure, it was easy to explain it as an exemplary act of protection by the God Yhwh.

Nevertheless, there was strong Assyrian domination within Syria-Palestine, as well as the introduction of Assyrian objects and deities into the temple in Jerusalem, which must have caused a problem. How could the people of Judah explain the cohabitation of Yhwh and his court with the representatives and symbols of the Assyrian religion?

It was thus that the "Yhwh alone" party came into being in the South, in the context of anti-Assyrian resistance. Around 630, the Assyrian Empire faded under the threat of another emerging great power, Babylon. It is within this context that King Josiah accedes to the throne, supported by the rural aristocracy who were traditionally hostile to the idea of a royal Yhwh. Josiah was surrounded by a group of counselors who urged him to undertake a kind of political and religious reform. This group is called by modern scholars the "Deuteronomists," because they were responsible for writing the first book of Deuteronomy, which advocates the worship of Yhwh alone. The Deuteronomists put their readers on guard against the worship of other gods. According to 2 Kings 22–23, Josiah established a policy of centralization. The temple in Jerusalem was declared the only legitimate sanctuary and all symbols and statues that were considered non-Yahwistic were suppressed. On the political level, anti-Assyrian measures were introduced, and on the religious level, the first attempt to formalize the worship of Yhwh alone was established, rejecting all other deities. But Josiah's reforms were not much of an influence in the short term. Neither Jeremiah nor Ezekiel refers to them. In 609, Josiah was killed by the Egyptian king, having come to the aid of the Assyrians, and in Judah there was probably a return to the traditional national religion during the last decades preceding the destruction of Jerusalem by the Babylonians in 587.

The Babylonian Exile: A Turning Point for Faith in Yhwh

It is difficult to imagine the impact provoked by the destruction of Jerusalem and the deportation of a group of very prominent Judeans to Mesopotamia. In fact, the events of 597–587 BC destroyed the pillars on which rested the worship of a national god at the time of the monarchy:

- The king of Judah was dethroned and would die in exile in Babylon.
- The temple in Jerusalem, symbol of God's presence, was destroyed.
- The country of Judah came under the direct rule of Babylon.

Therefore, the identity of the Judean people and their God could no longer be established through the traditional cultural and political institutions. Other ways had to be found that would allow them to express who Yhwh was; consequently, it was necessary to go beyond the idea of a pantheon with Yhwh as the national god. In fact, if they wanted to continue to think in terms of a national deity, they would have to admit that Yhwh had been beaten by Marduk, the patron god of the Babylonians. Besides, it is highly probable that some Judeans in exile in Babylon had already tried to go over to the worship of Marduk, since the processions organized in his honor would have made an impression on more than one exile. In order to maintain faith in the God of Israel, that faith had to be radically rethought. It is in response to this crisis that a new, many-faceted image of Yhwh takes shape.

God in the Deuteronomistic Context

First of all, the prophetic utterances about God that affirmed his demands and his judgments, and that up to now had remained marginal, grew in "official" significance in the context of the destruction of Jerusalem in 587. In order to find an analogous phenomenon, we could imagine the reaction of a society that had survived a major nuclear disaster. People would set out to find all the writings published by antinuclear movements throughout the preceding years and would rush to canonize them. Thus, a group of intellectuals undertook to edit a body of literature containing certain prophetic books; at the same time, this same group drew up a complete history of Israel from Moses down to the destruction of the Kingdom of Judah. Their work is called the "Deuteronomist history,"[11] since the theology of these books is largely inspired by Deuteronomy. For the Deuteronomists, the disaster of the exile comes about because the people and their kings are not willing to worship the God of Israel alone and obey his laws. So, the fall of Jerusalem does not demonstrate the weakness of Yhwh; it is a self-induced punishment for the disobedience of his people (see 2 Kgs 24:2–4). As a result, Yhwh's superiority over the Assyrian and Babylonian deities is affirmed, but in being affirmed, Yhwh is presented with their characteristics: as a great warrior, driven by a spirit of vengeance against his enemies.

God in the Priestly Context

Among the priests in exile, there developed another explanation of the God of Israel, which was more peaceable than that of their Deuteronomist colleagues. For the priests, it was more about the issue of how to worship God without the traditional structures. This resulted in their editing a document that begins with the story of Creation in Genesis 1. This narrative concludes with the institution of the Sabbath (Gen 2:1–3), in contrast to other cosmogonies of the time that end with the building of a physical sanctuary. The sacred space, then, is turned into a sacred time, which means that God can be worshipped through a liturgy that focuses more on time rather than place. For a people who have lost their temple, this is indispensible.

Even if the institutions of the monarchy have collapsed, the priestly authors remain convinced that access to God can be gained only through some kind of mediation, which should be ensured by the clergy. So we find an interesting law at the heart of the priestly document (in Exodus 25 to 40, and in the first part of the Book of Leviticus) that is contrary to a law of Deuteronomy concerning themes relating to worship, such as sacrifices, feast days, and the equipment within the sanctuary, which they were hurrying to rebuild.

In this way, the priestly narrative actively participates in the redefinition of the identity of the Jewish people and their God. The priestly authors, in fact, propose new institutions to replace those that were linked to the worship of God during the monarchy. They insist on the *Sabbath*, which is inscribed in the order of Creation itself; *circumcision*, which is introduced through the covenant with Abraham in Genesis 17; *Passover*, which is transformed from a royal to a family ritual by the formal recollection of the exodus from Egypt; and the observance of *food laws*, which are first revealed in the covenant with Noah after the flood and laid down in detail in the Book of Leviticus. It is worth stressing that all these institutions regulate the relationship between Yhwh and Israel in terms of mobility; that is to say, they are applicable just as much within their homeland as outside of it: during the exile or in diaspora.

For the priestly writers, the God of Israel is the God of all humanity. He wills the well-being and the blessing of all human beings. Thus, the covenant with Noah, whose sign is the rainbow, is valid for all the peoples who are descendants of Noah. And the covenant with Abraham, whose sign is circumcision, includes Ishmael, the ancestor of the Arab tribes. Even so, this God who is so universal has characteristics that seem to us perhaps less reassuring. Thus, in the priestly version of the Exodus, it is God who hardens Pharaoh's heart by not giving him the opportunity to convert. In the priestly document, Yhwh is certainly a universal God, but the liberation of Israel from Egypt is understood as a fight against the gods of Egypt (Exod 12:12).

God according to Deutero-Isaiah

The first to put forward a clear monotheist theory is undoubtedly an anonymous prophet called Deutero-Isaiah (or "Second Isaiah"), whose oracles are contained in the second part of the Book of Isaiah (chapters 40 to 55). Here,

Yhwh is acknowledged as the only God, while all other gods are merely imaginary: "I am the first and I am the last; / besides me there is no god" (Isa 44:6). The gods of the peoples, even those of the victors, are nothing but idols, made of "firewood" (44:17). And in 44:9 we read: "All who make idols are nothing, and the things they delight in do not profit; their witnesses neither see nor know." It is here that the monotheism of the Old Testament finds its theological fulfillment, expressed with impact and power, and at a time when things hardly look favorable for affirming the sovereignty of Yhwh. But it is at this crisis point (exile and occupation) that the monotheist credo emerges. In Second Isaiah, the Persian king Cyrus is presented as a messiah sent from Yhwh, a servant whom he has sent to free his people.

Therefore, it is from the time of the exile onward that the monotheist faith is fully expressed, confessing one God, who is creator of the world and governor of the destiny of the whole of humanity, but who nevertheless enjoys a special relationship with Israel, his chosen people. Historians observe that this evolution of the Yahwist faith was not immediately accepted by everyone. We only need remember the Jewish colony at Elephantine, in the south of Egypt, which in the fifth century BC still worshipped YHWH as one of a triad of deities.

The Great Synthesis

The various perspectives on God as they emerged in the last decades of the Kingdom of Judah and during the Babylonian and Persian eras coexist in the same Bible with more archaic, or, indeed, obscure, representations. Why?

The Hebrew Bible does not contain a single, unified, non-contradictory set of teachings about God. On the contrary, its writings offer a synthesis of different statements on

Yhwh and his people. The synthesis first appears with the publication of the Torah, the Pentateuch, as the official document of Judaism during the Persian era. The Persians were very tolerant toward religions and allowed great autonomy to the populations that were integrated into the empire. Some have even suggested that the Persians encouraged the gathering and the compilation of the religious traditions of the various peoples they ruled, although this is debated. However, what is certain is that, during the Persian era, the Judean intellectuals felt again the need to gather and to promulgate the founding documents of their religion. It was the Babylonian deportees who took the initiative to publish the Torah. The prophet Ezra, who was both a scribe and a priest, arrives in Jerusalem as the person in charge of the restoration of Jewish worship, and he proclaims the Law of the "God of heaven" (Ezra 7:12). It is interesting to note that "God of heaven" could refer to Yhwh whose law Ezra is proclaiming, but is also the title applied to Ahura-Mazda, the high god of the Persians. Following the Jewish tradition, the Law promulgated by Ezra could be identified as the Pentateuch or an early form of the Pentateuch. Therefore, it is evident that the Pentateuch, as the sole Law of Judaism, reflects the different theological tendencies of the Jewish communities in Babylon, Egypt, and Judea itself. This principle is equally valid for the second and third parts of the Old Testament canon, the Prophets and the Writings.

This new emphasis in Judaism focuses on the Law, but the Law is not a closed book; it is a collection that maintains all the diversity of experience that the Hebrew people have had with their God. Yhwh is both the God worshipped since the origins of humanity (Gen 4:26), and the God who has revealed his name to mankind beginning with Moses (Exod 3). Yhwh is both the God who enters into contact with the Arabs, the Philistines, and the Egyptians (in the Book of Genesis), but also the God who forbids Israel from having contact with other peoples, even ordering their extermination (for example, in certain passages in the Book of Deuteronomy). Yhwh is both a merciful God and a God who becomes angry.

All these images of God intersect with one another, and anyone who wishes to understand the Hebrew Bible must understand this interplay of images, as well as understand the different narratives of the God of the Old Testament.

THE NAME OF GOD IN THE OLD TESTAMENT

We have already seen how in the Old Testament God has a name, which, since the fourth or third century BC, Jews have refused to say aloud. This refusal is explained by the fact that it was inconceivable that the one and only God could be invoked through a proper name; there are also magical practices linked to the invocation of the name of Yhwh that they wanted to combat. In place of Yhwh, "Adonai" was used, or "(My) Lord" (a substitute that can be found in several English translations of the Bible). This practice is attested in the Greek translation of the Pentateuch, which renders the tetragram, the four letters of the divine name, mostly by the term *kurios*. Nowadays Judaism principally uses the substitute *ha-shem*, "the Name (blessed be he)" or "the Holy Name."

But What Does the Name *Yhwh* Mean?

The God of Israel has a proper name like all the gods of the ancient Near East. A proper name is used to mark, designate, or distinguish someone in relation to others, but it also helps to indicate contact with someone. In antiquity, the idea of naming someone or something is often found in the context of creation. So the Babylonian creation epic called *Enuma Elish* begins with the words "When the heavens above had not yet been named" to describe the state of the world before creation, in a similar way to Genesis 1:1–2. In Genesis 1, when God creates the different elements, he names them, and in Genesis 2, the man "participates" in creation by giving names to all the animals. The act of "naming," therefore, could be understood as an act of power. It is in order to avoid interfering in a power that is rightfully God's alone that Judaism does not speak the name of its God.

In order to determine the original pronunciation of the tetragrammaton (the four consonants, Y-H-W-H, that traditionally denote the name of God in Hebrew and that are written without vowels), we could look at some proper Hebrew names, such as Yirmeyahu (Jeremiah) or Yeshayahu (Isaiah), which appear to contain a short form of the name of God within them. This would make it plausible that the name of the God of Israel was pronounced Yahu or Yaho. The more traditional pronunciation of Yahweh, which can also be found in a number of English translations of the Bible, is based principally on some transcriptions of the divine name into Greek letters by the Fathers of the Church (such as Theodoret of Cyrus and Clement of Alexandria).

THE INTERPRETATION OF THE NAME *YHWH*

Although the word *Yhwh* occurs throughout the Hebrew Bible, only one passage attempts an explanation of its meaning: Exodus 3:12–15. These verses can be found in the narrative of the calling of Moses, where God is addressing Moses' objections to being sent back to Egypt to announce God's plan of liberation to the enslaved Israelites. First God promises to help Moses, saying: *'ehyeh 'imka* ("I will be with you"; Exod 3:12). Moses makes a second objection, that he does not know what name to use when telling the Israelites about God (Exod 3:13). Then God responds, not with his name, but with a kind of wordplay: *'ehyeh 'asher 'ehyeh*—which means, "I am who I am," or, "I will be who I will be," or, "I am who I will be" (Exod 3:14). This "response" evidently presupposes that the reader of the narrative knows the name of Yhwh. For the author of Exodus 3:14, therefore, this name is linked to a verb that means "to be" or "to become."

But how are we to understand the way in which God presents himself here?

Some commentators, notably Martin Buber, state that this is not a revelation of the name, but a concealment. God refuses to divulge his name, in essence saying: "I am who I am, and that does not concern you." However, taken literally, this interpretation poses a problem, since in Exodus 3:15, God presents himself to Moses as Yhwh, God of his fathers.

We must also stress the fact that *'ehyeh 'asher 'ehyeh* shows the dynamic aspect of the God of Israel. God is not a *deus otiosus*, a "lazy god," withdrawn from the affairs of the world; Yhwh is a God who intervenes, who seeks a relationship. He wants to be there, to be with someone. In the context of Exodus 3:12, the name of Yhwh could be understood as a promise. By being a promise, he escapes the control of man; it is in this sense that the reluctance of Yhwh to reveal himself should be understood.

The Problem of the Name's Etymology

According to the biblical account, the name Yhwh has its origin in the verbal form *hayah*—"to be." Some, therefore, think that Yhwh simply means "he who is" or, indeed, "he who makes things be," that is, the creator. That, at least, is one theological interpretation that goes some way toward explaining Exodus 3:14, but it is not very likely that that was the initial meaning of the name Yhwh.

The name Yahweh is perhaps formed based on the root *h-w-y*, which means "to blow" (of the wind). It would then be translated as "he who blows, who brings the wind."[12] Such a name also strongly corresponds to the function of a "storm god," and we have seen in our historical overview that Yhwh was closely associated with this status. But we can also see that this idea had become less prominent by the time Yhwh was declared to be the only God.

The Origin of *Yhwh*

According to Exodus 3, the name of Yhwh was not known to the Hebrews before the exodus from Egypt (see also Hos 12 and Ezek 20). The priestly variant[13] of the calling of Moses in chapter 6 of the Book of Exodus says the same. In Exodus 6:3, God presents himself to Moses saying: "I appeared to Abraham, Isaac, and Jacob as El Shaddai [the "powerful God" or the "God of the fields"], but under my name 'Yhwh,' I did not make myself known to them." These texts demonstrate clearly the idea that Yhwh has not been the God of Israel from the beginning. Also, the theophoric name Israel—which perhaps means "God combats" or "God rules"—is formed containing the word *El*—the great Canaanite God—and not containing the name Yhwh.

Therefore, we could say that Israel existed even before it confessed Yhwh to be its God.

It follows then that Yhwh is not a "native" god in Syria-Palestine. He is also absent from all the pantheons, at least in the texts known to us today. According to the biblical witnesses, Yhwh comes from the south: from Edom in Judges 5:4; from Teman in Arabia in Obadiah 3:3; from Sinai in Psalm 68:9. Yhwh, therefore, has not always been the God of Israel, and the encounter of Yhwh and his people is related in one way or another with the Hebrews in Egypt, as stated by the prophet Hosea (Hos 12:10).

This means that the relationship between Israel and its God is the fruit of an encounter, an event, reflected in the biblical narratives of the divine revelation on Sinai. This initial encounter, which for the historian remains rather obscure, comes at the start of a long history that eventually resulted in the Old Testament. In the course of that history, the biblical texts often present a Yhwh who appears shocking to us. Let us try now to better understand some of these texts about Yhwh that raise so many questions.

CHAPTER ONE

IS GOD MALE?

A four-year-old girl went to her parish priest and asked him: "Father, is God a man?" The priest answered: "No, child, God is not a man." She replied, "Then why do we call God our Father?" A small child's innocent question humorously conveys the difficulty we can have in understanding God.[1]

How can human beings speak about a God who transcends them, a God who remains elusive? If God is God, there is no human category that we can use to talk about him adequately. It is no wonder, then, that some theologians and philosophers have declared themselves to be in favor of a theology of silence, and to refrain from speculation on the being and attributes of God.

However, Judaism and Christianity both have their respective foundations in the belief that God intervenes in human affairs and communicates with them, that God cares about humankind and the world. For this reason, the authors of the Old Testament (just like those of the New Testament) have written down the traditions concerning this God in order to pass them on to future generations. In doing so, they felt compelled to use human concepts when speaking about God.

In the Bible, Yhwh is obviously described as if he were masculine. All the verbal forms that the Old Testament uses to describe the actions of God are masculine. A historian of religions would explain the logic of this naming convention by pointing out that Yhwh was originally revered as a baal, a storm god with necessarily masculine characteristics. We could add that during the Persian and Greek periods when the religious traditions of Israel were written down, Judaism was dominated by priests and scribes who were all men.

We do not need to dwell long on the fact that in popular and artistic imagery, the God of the Bible was almost always represented as an old man with a beard who was nonetheless powerful. This concept is seen most clearly in the works of Michelangelo.

In the wake of the feminist movement, theologians have strongly criticized the male concept of God. For some, the "macho" representation of Yhwh comes from a bad interpretation of the Old Testament; others, by contrast, believe that the whole Bible and its God do nothing but legitimize patriarchal power. They suggest that we should rediscover goddess worship and send the God of the Old Testament into exile.

I do not feel qualified to elaborate on this question, and I would not be able to intervene directly in the debate between the various feminist theologies. However, I do think it would be useful to conduct an investigation into the different forms under which the "masculinity" of Yhwh is represented in the Old Testament. Such an undertaking must necessarily deal with the feminine aspects on the worship of Yhwh: Did ancient Israel have goddesses? Or does the Bible exclude all integration of femininity from theological discussion? We will see that the Old Testament does not provide an incisive answer to these questions. It confronts us, instead, with different concepts of the "sex" of Yhwh, which are explained through the evolution of the

Old Testament faith, but also through the diversity of theological approaches in the Old Testament.

MALE IMAGES OF YHWH

It is obvious that most of the Old Testament texts that speak of God present him, whether consciously or not, as a man. Thus, Moses speaks to God face to face "as one would speak man to man" (Exod 33:1). In the story of the fall, which represents God walking in the garden enjoying the evening breeze (Gen 3:8), the author views Yhwh as a rural aristocrat or a king inspecting his property. Similarly, God can often be identified with his messengers (*mal'ak*), who, in the Old Testament, are always male. In this case, the masculinity of Yhwh is presupposed. There are other images that conceptualize this.

YHWH AS KING

More than fifty texts in the Old Testament present Yhwh as a king. Some of these probably date from the royal era and reflect the worship of Yhwh as a national God (cf. Isa 6:1; 1 Kgs 22:19). We can imagine Yhwh and his heavenly court just like the earthly royalty that God founds and legitimizes.

Psalm 93 begins like this:

The LORD is king, he is robed in majesty;
    the LORD is robed, he is girded with strength.
He has established the world; it shall never be moved;
    your throne is established from of old;
    you are from everlasting. (Ps 93:1–2)

DARK GOD

As king, God must above all guarantee order and peace for his realm, that is, for his creation. The royal psalms often describe Yhwh in the act of fighting against aquatic monsters that represent the forces of chaos. The Psalmist is using here a traditional concept in the ancient Near East according to which the principal deity is proclaimed king after having vanquished the primordial monsters (like Baal in Ugarit, or Marduk in Babylon). This fight is part of both the creation of the world and its maintenance. A similar representation clearly appears in Psalm 74, which is based on the Ugaritic myth of the victory of Baal over the god of the sea and his acolytes:

> Yet God my King is from of old,
>   working salvation in the earth.
> You divided the sea by your might;
>   you broke the heads of the dragons in the waters.
> You crushed the heads of Leviathan;
>   you gave him as food for the creatures of the
>   wilderness." (Ps 74:12–14)

We also find the same concept in Psalm 89 (vv 10–11), where it is combined with the election of David, the founder of the Judean dynasty (v 4). We see in passing that the idea of the God-king combating chaos can also be found in the New Testament. In the passage on the "calming of the storm" (Mark 4:35–41), the lordship of Jesus is demonstrated by the fact that he threatens the wind and the sea, as Yhwh does in the psalms (e.g., 65:8; 89:10).

This description of Yhwh as king, therefore, promotes a theology of the sovereignty of the God of Israel: "Who among the heavenly beings is like the LORD?" (Ps 89:6). As king, Yhwh protects his country and his temple (Ps 48), and gives prosperity to the earthly king and his people.

The royal image of Yhwh certainly presupposes the image of a male God. But it is the statement that God protects his people and his creation[2] that comes to the foreground. In the first millennium BC, it was rightly the royal image that best symbolized the functions of protection and safeguarding. It remains to be seen whether this still holds true today.

YHWH AS SPOUSE OR LOVER

In several of the prophetic books, notably in the books of Hosea, Jeremiah, and Ezekiel, Yhwh is defined as the husband or lover of his people. In the oracles of judgment, Israel appears then as an unfaithful woman who deceives her husband, Yhwh, by prostituting herself with other gods: "[She] went after her lovers, and forgot me, says the LORD" (Hos 2:13). Other texts compare Israel and Judah to sisters who are unfaithful and deceive Yhwh, their legitimate spouse, an image that evidently presupposes the practice of polygamy in ancient Israel. Thus we have, for example:

> Have you seen what she did, that faithless one, Israel, how she went up on every high hill and under every green tree, and played the whore there? And I thought, "After she has done all this she will return to me"; but she did not return, and her false sister Judah saw it. She saw that for all the adulteries of that faithless one, Israel, I had sent her away with a decree of divorce; yet her false sister Judah did not fear, but she too went and played the whore. (Jer 3:6–8)

The same idea is further developed in Ezekiel 16 and contains descriptions that are more shocking for the contemporary reader. In order to punish the unfaithful wife described as a prostitute, Yhwh arranges for her to be humiliated, stripped naked, and raped by all of her former lovers (vv 37–38). This text brings together the worst of male fantasies and attributes them to God.

In the prophetic oracles, the roles are clearly distributed: Yhwh is the husband, master, and proprietor (in Hebrew, it is the same word) of his wife, who thinks only of deceiving him. Some feminist theologians see in this kind of representation the theological legitimization of the patriarchy. The corollary of these prophetic accusations may be found in the passages that describe the origins of the relationship between Yhwh and his people as an encounter between two lovers: there are even some erotic elements that are quite evident in these descriptions:

> Therefore, I will now allure her,
>> and bring her into the wilderness,
>> and speak tenderly to her.[3]
> From there I will give her her vineyards,
>> and make the Valley of Achor a door of hope.
> There she shall respond as in the days of her youth,
>> as at the time when she came out of the land of
>> Egypt. (Hos 2:14–15)

Israel's time in the desert is described as being the honeymoon between Yhwh and his fiancée:

> I remember the devotion of your youth,
>> your love as a bride,
> how you followed me in the wilderness,
>> in a land not sown. (Jer 2:2)

In all these passages, the insistence on the amorous relationship between Yhwh and Israel is particularly marked, and reveals the passion that God has for his people. God is so much in love with his people that he necessarily becomes jealous of anyone who can turn his people from that love. We could say that God's passion for Israel—indeed, for all his creation—constitutes a central point, if not *the* central point, of the biblical message.

In order to express this message, the image of amorous human passion is used. In the context of the ancient Near East, there was no alternative but to give Yhwh the role of the man and Israel that of the woman. In these passages, the masculine quality of Yhwh is built into the relational context. This brings up a question about the worship of Yhwh: Was he worshipped as a male God?

YHWH AND HIS ASHERAH

As we have seen, Yhwh was worshipped as the national God during the period of the monarchy. This cult was celebrated in the royal temples in Jerusalem in the south, in Bethel and Dan in the north, and in various other sanctuaries. But we must make a distinction here between official religion and popular religion, and raise the question of the worship of Yhwh "in the provinces." The Old Testament itself attests to the existence of *bamôt*, sanctuaries located on hills and, in most cases, in the open air. Even Solomon visited one of these sanctuaries that was at Gibeon, where he received a divine message in a dream (1 Kgs 3).[4]

Both archaeology and biblical texts indicate that on these high places, cut stones were placed to a height of three meters or more. These stones, called *mazzebot*, were apparently in phallic form and symbolized one of the male deities. These were accompanied by wooden posts, called *asherot*, which represented female deities. The name *Asherah*

31

is the Hebrew form of *Athirat,* a goddess with a strong presence in the Canaanite pantheons (above all at Ugarit).

Is this worship of Asherah in the form of sacred posts—which is strongly opposed in the Bible, notably in Deuteronomy and the Deuteronomistic literature—limited exclusively to pagan, and not Yahwist, worship?

Exegetes have long insisted on the fact that Yhwh is a celibate God and that, consequently, the sexual aspect, which had a strong impact on Canaanite religions, played no part in the Yahwist religion. However, some religious historians have raised doubts regarding the concept of a national god without women or mistresses. Archaeological finds confirm the association of Yhwh with a goddess.

Khirbet el-Qom Inscription

In Khirbet el-Qom, a place located 14 kilometers (8.7 miles) west of Hebron, there are tomb inscriptions that date

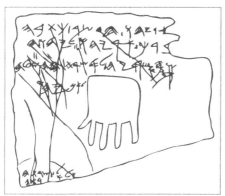

Fig. 1. Khirbet el-Qom inscription

from 750 to 700 BC. Deciphering the exact meaning of the inscriptions is rather difficult, but there is no doubt about the sense of them. The one shown here (Fig. 1) could be translated as: "Ourihaju, the rich, wrote it. Blessed be Ouriyahu by Yhwh;[5] from his enemies he saves by his Asherah." In this inscription, we find Yhwh linked with Asherah. We find this same association, in an even more spectacular way, at another site.

Kuntillet Ajrud Inscription

This site is 50 km southeast of Qadesh-Barnea in the Negev desert. It was investigated between 1975 and 1976 while Israel occupied the Sinai peninsula. The remains of a construction dating from the eighth century BC were discovered. It was perhaps a sanctuary frequented by pilgrims. Others see it as a kind of school, which, being in the middle of the desert, seems somewhat improbable. More likely, it was a relay station, a sort of hotel, as can be seen by some traces left by travelers. In fact, in several places there are graffiti and inscriptions on the walls, but also on jugs, called *pithoi*, done in red ink.

The most famous inscription (Fig. 2) runs as follows: "Word of…Speaks so to Yehal [el] and to Yo'ash…: I bless you by Yhwh of Samaria and by his Asherah." Asherah clearly appears here as the goddess associated with the God of Israel.

Fig. 2. Graffiti at Kuntillet 'Ajrud,
accompanied by representations of deities

The inscription is accompanied by a drawing showing two people in the foreground (seemingly masculine) and in the background probably a female playing a musical instrument. Interpreting this drawing poses a number of problems.

33

An Israelite scholar, M. Gilula, suggests that we identify the person on the left as Yhwh, since, according to him, it has bovine characteristics. The figure on the right would then represent Asherah, whose image, in a later act of censure, was "masculinized" by the addition of a penis.

This interpretation is, however, highly speculative. Many exegetes think that the double figure represents the Egyptian god Bes, who appeared often in the form of twins. So what about the person playing the lyre? Is this simply a male or female musician, or is it Asherah seated on a throne? The latter theory poses problems: the gender of the person is not clear and in mythological texts, Asherah does not appear as a musician goddess. There is therefore a strong possibility that there is no relationship between the inscriptions and the drawings.

However, we could ask whether the paintings found on the *other* side of the jug could be a representation of Asherah (Fig. 3). Judith Hadley, a specialist in this area, has theorized that the stylized tree found there could be the symbol of Asherah.[6] This would also explain the presence of the

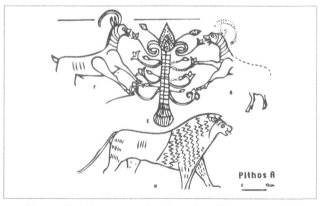

Fig. 3. Paintings on a jug found at Kuntillet 'Ajrud

lion, which is often said to be the goddess's favorite animal.

In any case, it is evident that in the inscription, the faithful are making an appeal to a divine couple: Yhwh and his Asherah. Some scholars have attempted to minimize this fact by arguing that here *ashera* is not a proper name, but instead designates an object of worship (a stylized tree); however, this changes absolutely nothing, since the deity and his symbol are inseparable. Recently Israeli specialists Nadav Na'aman and Nuri Lissovsky have put forward the idea that Kuntillet 'Ajrud was one of the main sanctuaries of the goddess Asherah.[7]

Fig. 4. The Ta'anakh object of worship

There is another archaeological find that perhaps allows us to establish a link between Yhwh and Asherah; it is a kind of censer found in 1968 at Ta'anakh in the southern part of the Jezreel Valley in Galilee (Fig. 4). This object, which dates from the tenth or ninth century BC, shows four segments. The two upper segments show a stylized tree and a solar disc accompanied undoubtedly by a horse (cf. 2 Kgs 23:11); it is very probable that here we are dealing with the symbols of Asherah and Yhwh. In that case, the object's two lower segments could relate to those symbols. Again according to Hadley, the female deity at the bottom corresponds to the figure of Asherah. Hadley has deduced that the opening guarded by two sphinxes could therefore be a way of symbolizing the presence of Yhwh, not by an image, but by the smoke escaping from the hole, which recalls the divine manifestations such as those described in the episode of Moses on Mount Sinai (Exod 19ff).

Biblical Attestations

We have to conclude that during the time of the monarchy, Yhwh was sometimes worshipped in association with Asherah. Therefore, does the worship of Yhwh have to be seen exclusively in the context of popular religion, with only the unofficial or private characteristics found in the inscriptions? No, it is possible that the cult of the couple "Yhwh and Asherah" was also part of the theology of the "official sanctuaries" during the period of the monarchy. This suggestion is corroborated by certain biblical texts. In First Kings 18:4, we read how King Hezekiah cut down an *asherah* of the temple, which necessarily presupposes that the goddess was already present in the sanctuary. Similarly, Manasseh restored to the temple an *asherah* that had been rejected through the reforms of Hezekiah (2 Kgs 21:3, 6, 7). It is evident, therefore, that during the time of the monarchy there had been symbols linked to the worship of a female partner to Yhwh, his consort, in the great national sanctuaries (a consort is a divine female figure of lower rank, seated beside a more influential deity). It is at the point at which the sanctuaries are destroyed and questioned that the concept of a male Yhwh accompanied by a goddess becomes unacceptable.

Nevertheless, we should note that the worship of a goddess called the "Queen of Heaven" was still very widespread at the time of the Babylonian exile. It was a cult in which women apparently played a central ritual role in making cakes for the goddess. Two passages from the Book of Jeremiah, passed down to us by the Deuteronomistic editors, severely criticize the cult. Chapter 44 is put forward as a discourse by Jeremiah to those who fled to Egypt to escape the Babylonians. The prophet explains to these refugee Judeans that the disaster overcame them because they were constantly worshipping other gods. The recipients of this criticism strongly contest this interpretation of the fall of Jerusalem, and emphasize that by worshipping the Queen of Heaven they were just doing what they had always done, and that disaster befell them when they had *stopped* making offerings to her:

> Instead, we will [again] do everything that we have vowed, make offerings to the queen of heaven and pour out libations to her, just as we and our ancestors, our kings and our officials, used to do in the towns of Judah and in the streets of Jerusalem. We used to have plenty of food, and prospered, and saw no misfortune. But from the time we stopped making offerings to the queen of heaven and pouring out libations to her, we have lacked everything and have perished by the sword and by famine. (Jer 44:17–18)

According to this argument, it is the prohibition of the cult of the goddess (through the reforms of Josiah?) that has rightly provoked all these catastrophes.

The implication is that the abolition of the cult of the Queen of Heaven, who is probably Asherah,[8] was still being hotly debated within Judaism in the sixth to the fifth centuries BC. For the record, we should note that the cult itself survived in several Christian denominations, since it is Mary who is called *Regina caeli* ("Queen of Heaven").

The Jewish community at Elephantine, as we have already seen, continued to associate a goddess with Yhwh (Yaho), again in the fifth century BC. In this community an oath was sworn by "the god Yaho, by the temple, and by the

Anat of Yaho." Yaho certainly remains the principal god and the sanctuary of the colony is his temple, but he is accompanied by Anat, a matriarchal goddess.

What happens when monotheism becomes the fundamental factor in Judaism's identity and, so to speak, in the "identity of God"? What becomes of the feminine principle when we speak of the one and only God? We could receive the impression that God definitely becomes the patriarch, since from this point on, addressing Yhwh as "father" takes on a certain importance.

GOD AS FATHER

Calling a god "father" is far from being just a biblical phenomenon. In the texts from Ugarit, the God El receives the title "Father of Humanity." In the Old Testament, we find certain proper names that include the element 'ab, meaning "father." For example, there are Abijah and Joab, meaning "Yhwh is father," and also Abram, meaning "the Father [the deity] is exalted."

The oldest texts that speak about Yhwh as father refer to the king, and the God-king relationship is compared to the father-son relationship. In his dynastic promise to David, God says about David's son and successor Solomon: "I will be a father to him, and he shall be a son to me" (2 Sam 7:14).

The other texts that speak of Yhwh as father—some fifteen in the Bible—all date from the period of the exile or even afterward. Here the designation of God as father is for a community, or for all the people who are considered sons of Yhwh. The first comment we can make about this is: the use of the term *father* to denote God reflects a democratization of the royal ideology; it is no longer the king alone who is the son of God, but the whole community that benefits from this relationship of proximity to God. This transfer of the use of the term *father* can be explained from the circumstances of the Babylonian exile: the institution of the monarchy had disappeared and the only structure that was still functioning was the family, within which the head role was that of the father. Instead of conceiving of God as a king, the people now think of God as a father.

Calling God "father" implies recognition of his authority. At the same time, this name expresses the idea of dependence: "Yet, O LORD, you are our Father; / we are the clay, and you are our potter; / we are all the work of your hand" (Isa 64:8). But it also expresses the privileged status of a believer who no longer has need of royal mediation in order to experience God's closeness: "You are children of the LORD your God" (Deut 14:1).

But invoking God as father could also be polemical, as in the case of Isaiah 63:7—64:11. This is a liturgy of lamentation that grew out of the worship during the Babylonian or Persian era. The following confession appears in this liturgy:

> For you are our father,
>> though Abraham does not know us
>> and Israel does not acknowledge us;
> you, O LORD, are our father;
>> our Redeemer from of old is your name."
>> (Isa 63:16)

We notice in this text a categorical refusal to apply the title of father to Abraham and Jacob (Israel). Calling God "father" is accompanied by a caution not to esteem the patriarchs too highly. Without doubt, the reason for the warning lies in the polemic against ancestor worship and necromancy that were continually practiced during the Persian period, as seen, for example, in Isaiah 65:6. We are dealing here with an author who is criticizing those who believed that the genealogical reference to the patriarchs would guarantee them a privileged relationship with God. Therefore, Yhwh alone becomes the father of Israel (cf. 64:7) as he is of the whole universe. This insistence on the fact that God alone is the father of his people also brings with it a distrust toward Israel's identifying itself genealogically: this is also found in the New Testament. So John the Baptist warns his listeners: "Do not presume to say to yourselves, 'We have Abraham as our ancestor'; for I tell you, God is able from these stones to raise up children to Abraham" (Matt 3:9). Thus, Christianity is able to take up again the monotheist message of the Hebrew Bible, especially as it appears in Isaiah, by affirming that we can use the name "father" for the God of the universe.

The sixth- and fifth-century-BC authors take the title "father" for granted. But was this their only way of speaking about God? Or, to rephrase the question: Did all the scribes during the Persian period think that the one God, the Creator of the universe, was an "exclusively male" God? This is not the case.

"MALE AND FEMALE HE CREATED THEM"

The account of Creation in Genesis 1, as written by the authors of the priestly tradition, has as its crowning moment the creation of man:

> Then God said, "Let us make humankind in our image, according to our likeness; and let them have dominion over the fish of the sea, and over the birds of the air, and over the cattle, and over

all the wild animals of the earth, and over every
creeping thing that creeps upon the earth."
So God created humankind in his image,
in the image of God he created them;
male and female he created them.
(Gen 1:26–27)

The affirmation that man is made in the image of God
has always provided a pivotal point for exegetes and theologians. A number of proposals have been put forward
aimed at understanding in what way man is made in the
image of his creator—intelligence, spirituality, language,
and so on. However, the above passage does not speak simply about one aspect of the human being, but of the human
being in its totality. The study of comparative religions can
help us understand this issue. In Egyptian texts, in particular, Pharaoh, the king, is often designated as the image of
God on earth. In this regard, the king is the mediator
between the world and God. In Genesis, chapter 1, which
affirms that every person is made in the image of God, we
find a process of democratization of the royal tradition that
is similar to what we have already described with respect to
the term *father* for God. Henceforth, *every person* is the representative of God on earth; that is, each person is responsible for Creation, which he or she must protect and allow to
prosper. This task falls to all of humanity, both male and
female: "male and female he created them." Here, the com-
plementarity and equality of the man and the woman are
affirmed in a forceful and solemn way. This text is quite
clear as to how human beings are the image of God.
According to Genesis 1, the man (male) alone cannot claim
to be the image of God. God finds his reflection just as
much in the woman as in the man. This affirmation by the
priestly authors allows us to see that, despite appearances,

41

the God of the Old Testament is not the bearded and over-bearing patriarch who is usually imagined or caricatured. According to Genesis 1, God has within himself an image that is feminine just as much as it is masculine. We can, therefore, continue our investigation by asking whether feminine traits of Yhwh emerge from these texts.

DOES GOD HAVE FEMININE CHARACTERISTICS?

If God often appears warlike and violent, he is at the same time merciful and slow to anger (see, e.g., Exod 34:6). But can we claim that mercy is a feminine characteristic, while violence is a masculine one? That would lead us to perpetuate some preconceived notions on the distribution of roles between man and woman. We can, however, make the comment that the Hebrew word used to designate mercy is *rakhamim*, a word that comes from the root *r-kh-m*, meaning the maternal womb, the uterus. This definition led the French Jewish scholar André Chouraqui, in his transla-tion of the Old Testament, to replace the word *merciful* with the word *matricial*. These etymological speculations are not, however, entirely relevant when we are considering whether divine mercy can be a quality of God the father, as it is in Psalm 103: "As a father has compassion for his children, / so the LORD has compassion for those who fear him" (v 13). In fact, as scholar Jaques Briend says, "The origin of a term is not enough to determine its usage, whether feminine or masculine."[9] Rather, when speaking about God, we must look at more explicit texts that involve the semantic field of motherhood. And, indeed, there are such texts.

Let us return first to the "Song of Moses" (Deut 32). In this text, which is in fact a psalm, God appears in verse 6 as the father: "Is not he your father, who created you, / who made you and established you?" But verse 18 contains the following accusation: "You were unmindful of the Rock that bore you; / you forgot the God who gave you birth." The verb *kh-y-l* is specifically maternal, with a clearly feminine value, the exact meaning of which is "giving birth in pain" (cf. Ps 29:9; Isa 51:2). But the verb here is in the masculine form. For Deuteronomy 32, this means that God is not limited to the masculine. In the same sense, Psalm 90:2 describes the creation of the earth by God as a birth.

We must also mention the surprising passage in Numbers 11. Here we read how Moses complains against Yhwh because of the people's heavy burden: "Did I conceive all this people? Did I give birth to them, that you should say to me, 'Carry them in your bosom, as a nurse carries a sucking child?'" (v 12). The imagery Moses uses in questioning the divine order clearly comes out of the terminology of motherhood: conceiving, giving birth, carrying in the bosom a suckling child (the Hebrew word implies that it is a baby who is still being breast-fed). Therefore, through the comparisons used in this verse, God appears clearly as the mother of Israel.

It is in the second part of the Book of Isaiah that the maternal images for God are the most numerous. In Isaiah 49:15, God replies to the people who believe they have been forgotten, using the following words:

> Can a woman forget her nursing child,
>   or show no compassion for the child of her womb?
> Even these may forget,
>   yet I will not forget you.

Therefore, the attitude of Yhwh toward Zion, which represents here the population that was not deported to Babylon and who feels far from God, is compared to the love a mother has for her children. The maternal reference is therefore obvious.

The statement in Isaiah 43:2 has the same sense:

Listen to me, O house of Jacob,
　　all the remnant of the house of Israel,
who have been borne by me from your birth,
　　carried from the womb.

In the third line, the words *borne by me* imply *borne by God*, and later in verse 4 we will find the same verb. According to this text, God looks after Israel like a mother looks after her children. He appears as a mother who has given birth to her son Jacob/Israel. The metaphor of giving birth is present in a similar way in Isaiah 42:14. In this verse, the people's exile is explained by the fact that God has remained inactive. But that time is over, and God will act in favor of his people. The beginning of this intervention is described in verse 14b, in this way: "Now I will cry out like a woman in labor, / I will gasp and pant." The deliverance of the exiled people is then presented as a new birth, which is in complete agreement with the theology of Deutero-Isaiah who describes the return from exile and the restoration of Israel as a new exodus and a new creation. The comparison is very bold: Yhwh is compared to a woman in the pains of childbirth. However, in the previous verse, this same Yhwh is presented as a "warrior…; / he cries out, he shouts aloud, / he shows himself mighty against his foes." Therefore, we see here an astonishing transformation of an all-powerful God, a warrior, into a maternal God who suffers—we could say, "who undergoes agony" for his people.

It is no coincidence that Isaiah, from chapter 40 on, abounds in maternal images.[10] As we have seen, this is the book in which the belief in one God, Creator of the world and Redeemer of Israel, is most powerfully expressed. If there is only one God, as Deutero-Isaiah states, then that God is at the same time father and mother. The fact remains, however, that even if the feminine metaphors are obvious, God is never actually called "mother," either in the Old or the New Testament. This could no doubt be explained by the sociocultural context in which biblical texts have their roots, but perhaps also by the fear that calling God "mother" would evoke the goddesses against whose worship the authors of the Persian period had been fighting. Today, circumstances have certainly changed and any theological reflection on the proper way of talking about God should revisit this issue. We have nothing but human language if we wish to speak about God. The image of God that we carry within ourselves is borne out by our personal experience and by our "religious socialization." This image may have to evolve if our ideas about his masculinity or femininity have become fixed. The risk of the traditional patriarchal interpretation, as with the "modern" feminist interpretation of God, is the same: we must guard against confining God within our own human conceptions.

Hosea 11:9 reminds us: "I am God and no mortal," and that is the reason that the Decalogue exhorts its recipients: "Do not make for yourself any image."

When we speak about God we find this tension: the need to speak about God using "images" and metaphors— knowing all the while that these are inadequate ways of speaking about a God who can be compared to no one or no thing (Isa 46:5).

CHAPTER 2

IS GOD CRUEL?

The great philosopher Emmanuel Kant (1724–1804) asked himself a question that is still relevant today: How can a human being be certain that it is God who speaks to him through the text of the Bible? Kant believed that there was no positive answer. On the contrary, he considered that, under certain conditions, a human being can only know when it is *not* God who is speaking to him. And, according to the philosopher, this is especially true when an action or a commandment that claims to be divine goes against the universal moral law, as in the case in Genesis 22, where God orders Abraham to sacrifice his own son. According to Kant, Abraham should have responded to this order in the following way:

> I am sure I should not kill my son, but I am not sure that you who are appearing to me at this moment are truly God.[1]

These comments are quite typical of how Enlightenment thought dealt with Old Testament passages that presented incomprehensible images of God. Why then does the Hebrew Bible seem to depict God as cruel? Many passages seem to describe a God who stands in opposition to humans. The collection of oracles by the prophets Amos,

Hosea, and Micah, for example, present judgments that are so cruel that they are more like a declaration of war by God against his people.

> So, I will press you down in your place,
>   just as a cart presses down
>   when it is full of sheaves. (Amos 2:13)

> Therefore thus says the LORD, the God of hosts:
> Because they have spoken this word,
> I am now making my words in your mouth a fire,
>   and this people wood, and the fire shall devour
>   them. (Jer 5:14)

However, these very difficult passages are written from the perspective of a specifically *prophetic* view of history. There is a reason why God manifests himself as an opponent. These judgments are explained by the social injustices and aberrations of worship that Yhwh, through his prophets and scribes, was criticizing.

Nevertheless, there are some cases where the God of the Old Testament shows hardness or cruelty in a "gratuitous" way, without humanity's culpability being established from the outset. There are some passages that provoke Kant's protests and that remain unacceptable to many of our contemporaries. How can God be so cruel, to the point where he seems to delight in putting his people to the test? Is it not the case that a God who requires or accepts the sacrifice of children is a bloodthirsty demon and not the God who creates and redeems? And how can the God of the Old Testament intend to kill those who believe themselves to be under his protection?

If we want to try to respond to these questions, we run at least two risks: that of adopting, a priori, a position of advocacy that would not take these texts seriously by claiming, for instance, that God could never harm those who believe in him; and that of losing ourselves in general considerations about God's "character" without looking seriously into what these texts have to say.

Let us conduct our investigation based on four texts. We will look at two stories of "infant" sacrifice commanded or tolerated by God. These are Genesis 22, the sacrifice of Abraham's son Isaac, which we have just mentioned, and Judges 11, the sacrifice of Jephthah's daughter. Next we will tackle two other narratives that seem to go even further, because here God appears to eliminate the human beings who are the recipients of his promises: Jacob in Genesis 32, and Moses in Exodus 4.

GOD AND HUMAN SACRIFICE

In many religions in antiquity, human sacrifices, and very often the sacrifice of children, were offered up in a moment of crisis, when a community could not find any other way of provoking the intervention of the deity in their favor. The Old Testament keeps track of such practices. The Second Book of Kings has the following account:

> When the king of Moab saw that the battle was going against him, he took with him seven hundred swordsmen to break through, opposite the king of Edom; but they could not. Then he took his firstborn son who was to succeed him, and offered him as a burnt offering on the wall. And great wrath came upon Israel, so they withdrew from him and returned to their own land. (3:26–27)

The scribes who provided this passage for us were certainly shocked by its contents. This explains the fact that these verses have been lightly "censored." However, what they have to say is quite clear: the king of Moab who was at war with Israel, in the absence of any other solution, offers up his son to Kemosh, the god of the Moabites. Apparently, according to the primitive text, the sacrifice provokes the wrath of Kemosh against the Israelites, who have to abandon their position. The text itself condemns this practice, since there is probably a suggestion that the Israelites were so disgusted by the Moabite king's action that they hastened to leave the territory.

In some texts of the laws of the Pentateuch, there are many prohibitions against human sacrifice, for example, Deuteronomy 18:10–12: "No one shall be found among you who makes a son or daughter pass through fire….For whoever does these things is abhorrent to the LORD" (see also Lev 20:1–2).

So, when God asks Abraham to offer his son as a holocaust, or when he accepts the fact that Jephthah sacrifices his daughter to him, is he not contradicting himself?

The "Testing" of Abraham

The text of Genesis 22:1–19, called the Aqedah in Jewish tradition, that is to say the "Binding of Isaac," is without doubt the best known episode in the whole story of Abraham (Gen 12–25). It has been amply commented on by Jewish and Christian theologians and has inspired many paintings by artists (for example, Rembrandt, Chagall, Dali), but also ironic or cynical remarks, such as, for example, those by Woody Allen.[2] In 1994, French television aired a TV movie on Abraham, and the scene with the sacrifice provoked a series of heated reactions, as evidenced by letters to the editor published in the newspaper *Le Monde*. One author wrote:

> A father prepares to slaughter his young son as an offering to an unknown but rather talkative god who, in a voice that comes from the clouds, orders him to carry out the killing in order to "test him." The father should have rebelled and refused point blank! It is this horror story that believers still glorify and that is responsible today for the slaughter of sheep that have to be willing victims.[3]

Let us take a fresh look at the passage that has provoked so much feeling.

> After these things God tested Abraham. He said to him, "Abraham!" And he said, "Here I am." He said, "Take your son, your only son Isaac, whom you love, and go to the land of Moriah, and bring him up there as a burnt offering on one of the mountains that I shall show you." So Abraham rose early in the morning, saddled his donkey, and took two of his young men with him, and his son Isaac; he cut the wood for the burnt offering, and set out and went to the place in the distance that God had shown him. On the third day Abraham looked up and saw the place far away. Then Abraham said to his young men, "Stay here with the donkey; the boy and I will go over there; we will worship, and then we will come back to you." Abraham took the wood of the burnt offering and laid it on his son Isaac, and he himself carried the fire and the knife. So the two of them

walked on together. Isaac said to his father Abraham, "Father!" And he said, "Here I am, my son." He said, "The fire and the wood are here, but where is the lamb for a burnt offering?" Abraham said, "God himself will provide the lamb for a burnt offering, my son." So the two of them walked on together.

When they came to the place that God had shown him, Abraham built an altar there and laid the wood in order. He bound his son Isaac, and laid him on the altar, on top of the wood. Then Abraham reached out his hand and took the knife to kill his son. But the angel of the LORD called to him from heaven, and said, "Abraham, Abraham!" And he said, "Here I am." He said, "Do not lay your hand on the boy or do anything to him; for now I know that you fear God, since you have not withheld your son, your only son, from me." And Abraham looked up and saw a ram, caught in a thicket by its horns. Abraham went and took the ram and offered it up as a burnt offering instead of his son. So Abraham called that place "The LORD will provide"; as it is said to this day, "On the mount of the LORD it shall be provided."

The angel of the LORD called to Abraham a second time from heaven, and said, "By myself I have sworn, says the LORD: Because you have done this, and have not withheld your son, your only son, I will indeed bless you, and I will make your offspring as numerous as the stars of heaven and as the sand that is on the seashore. And your offspring shall possess the gate of their enemies, and by your offspring shall all the nations of the earth gain blessing for themselves, because you have obeyed my voice." So Abraham returned to his young men, and they arose and went together to Beer-sheba; and Abraham lived at Beer-sheba. (Gen 22:1–19)

"After these things," meaning the previous events, God puts Abraham to the test, saying to him, "Take your son, your only son Isaac, whom you love, and go to the land of Moriah, and offer him there as a burnt offering on one of the mountains that I shall show you" (vv 1–2). In this passage, the word *God* could also be translated as "the divinity," since the Hebrew *elohim* takes the article, which in Biblical Hebrew often has the effect of making God more distant.

This introduction must be understood in connection to the previous events in the story of Abraham. Several times, God had made a promise of a son and many descendants to the infertile couple Abraham and Sarah, a promise that faced repeated obstacles: Sarah was taken into the harem of a foreign king (Gen 12 and 20); Abraham risked his life in going to war (Gen 14); the couple wanted to "force" the promise with Ishmael (Gen 16); Abraham (Gen 17) and Sarah (Gen 18) remained skeptical when God renewed the birth announcement. But at last the promise was accomplished in chapter 21 with the birth of Isaac. It is immediately after this account that God comes and delivers his command, thus calling into question the validity of his promise and his faithfulness. As one commentator has pointed out, Abraham, in Genesis 22, experiences a God who contradicts himself.[4]

Certainly, readers of this passage know more than Abraham, since the narrator reveals God's intention from the start (that God was merely "testing" the patriarch). Nevertheless, readers of the Bible find themselves in dramatic tension, as they cannot communicate to the main character, Abraham, what they know. This is a method often used in suspense movies. For example, in films by Alfred Hitchcock and other directors, the viewers know who the real culprit is, but they cannot intervene to warn the wrongly suspected hero of an evil plot.

However, in Genesis 22, the test seems more than cruel; it seems unbearable. We are not the first to have misgivings about this text. Many Jewish commentators have interpreted the command to sacrifice Isaac as coming not from God, but from Satan. Another Jewish interpretation has the devil intervening, but in order to prevent Abraham from obeying (cf. the "Bereshit Rabba" rabbinical commentary on Genesis). Satan would confront Abraham with a quote from the Torah: "Whoever sheds the blood of a human, by a human shall that person's blood be shed" (Gen 9:6). This plainly shows that the rabbis were well aware of the theological difficulties of God's command. A contemporary attempt to defuse the scandalous side of Genesis 22:1–2 was developed by French psychoanalyst Marie Balmary. According to her, Abraham totally misunderstood what God wanted to begin with, and so erroneously prepared to sacrifice his son Isaac. She takes up a comment made by Rashi (1040–1105), a Jewish exegete of the Middle Ages, who had noted that the literal translation of God's command is "to bring him [Isaac] up," and she concludes, as he does, that God never asked for a blood sacrifice from Abraham. She writes:

> If God asks for the immolation of Isaac the whole story is an extreme (and almost absurd) test....But if God did not ask Abraham for immolation but Abraham, himself, at first believed him to, then we are being presented with the unveiling

of Abraham's imagination and the transformation of his faith.[5]

According to this psychoanalytical reading, the event is a
cure, in which God heals Abraham of his poor understanding
of God. Such an interpretation is certainly less unpleasant,
but the fact is that it does not respect the genuinely shocking
nature of the story.[6] Also, the expression *to bring up* is used
throughout the whole Hebrew Bible as a technical term to
mean a "holocaust," a sacrifice that is completely burned and
the smoke of which rises up to God. Therefore, the command
addressed to Abraham is unambiguous, according to the narrator of Genesis 22. Abraham understood well what God was
asking. What is more, the biblical text is greatly understated.
We are never told what Abraham's reaction is, there is no
attempt to negotiate with God (as Abraham had done in Gen
18), nor does he demand explanations from God. He obeys
and acts: "Abraham rose early in the morning, saddled his
donkey, and took two of his young men with him, and his
son Isaac" (v 3).

The patriarch reacts exactly as he did at the start of his
relationship with God. In Genesis 12, God commands him:
"Go from your country...to the land that I will show you"
(v 1). God's command in the account of the Binding of Isaac
has the same structure: "Go to the land of Moriah...that I shall
show you" (v 2). These are the only two passages of Genesis
that are constructed with the insistent Hebrew expression *lek
leka* ("go, you").[7] The term *Moriah*, in Hebrew, contains an
allusion to the verb *to see*, which is also used in 12:1. In
Genesis 12, Abraham must abandon his past; in Gen 22 he
must sacrifice his future. And in both passages, he sets out.

What was Abraham thinking? What did he say to his
son Isaac? The biblical text remains silent; it is not interested in psychology. It is that silence that makes the unfold-

ing of the action almost unbearable. The silence is broken only once, when Isaac asks the question: "The fire and the wood are here, but where is the lamb for a burnt offering?" (v 7). And Abraham responds: "God himself will provide the lamb for a burnt offering, my son." This response is ambiguous. Did Abraham hope or know that the sacrifice of his son would not take place, or should we interpret those two last words, *my son*, as referring to the lamb—namely, "*You* are the lamb, my son"?

Abraham was not playing for time; he builds the altar and places his son on it—again, we are told nothing about Isaac's reaction—and stretches out his hand to kill him. Only at that point does the angel of the Lord intervene in order to, at last, bring things to a head. Abraham receives the title "God-fearing," and the boy is replaced by a ram that Abraham sees in a thicket. But despite this "happy ending" and a second announcement by the angel repeating the promises made to Abraham (which is, in the almost unanimous opinion of exegetes, an interpolation made by a later editor; namely, vv 15–18), we are scarcely tempted to heave a sigh of relief. At first Abraham's silence continues, then verse 19 quite simply notes that "Abraham returned to his young men [the boys who had accompanied them, but who had remained at the bottom of the hill], and they arose and went together to Beer-sheba." That final verse does not mention the return of Isaac, a fact that has greatly intrigued commentators. Jewish and Christian exegetes have postulated that Abraham really did sacrifice his son; in fact, if we read verse 19 directly following verse 10, we could sustain this hypothesis. However, this idea runs against all that the passage is attempting to say, as we shall see.

It is particularly significant that Genesis 22 is the only passage in the Abraham cycle where the patriarch offers a sacrifice. In the course of all his travels, he builds altars, but these are almost "presbyterian" altars since Abraham uses them exclusively for the purpose of "invoking the name of Yhwh." We get the impression that the authors of the passages in question want to distance themselves from sacrificial practices. Genesis 22 is certainly the only text that shows Abraham making a sacrifice and the sacrifice takes place on Mount Moriah. This is not a geographical name but a theological one, constructed using the verb *ra'ah*—"to see"—which is one of the key words of the narrative. According to the Second Book of Chronicles (2 Chr 3:1), Mount Moriah is the mountain of the temple in Jerusalem. The author of Genesis 22 probably already had this identification in mind. He therefore must have been aware of the Deuteronomistic theology according to which there was only one legitimate place for sacrificial worship, namely, the temple in Jerusalem.

If the author of the text is familiar with this theology, he can scarcely have written it before the sixth century BC. He would also have been aware that in extreme situations the people of Israel, like their neighbors, practiced human sacrifice. First and Second Kings criticize several kings for having put their children to death by fire. These barbaric practices, which are borne out by archaeology, seem to have been prevalent during the period when the Kingdom of Judah was in danger of being wiped out. How could these bloodthirsty customs be stopped? They could have been banned—this is the stance taken by the Law. But was prohibiting them enough? Would it not be more effective to explain to those who thought that human sacrifice was part of the worship of Yhwh that God disapproved of such practices? In Ezekiel 20:25, God makes a rather astonishing remark: "I gave them statutes that were not good and ordinances by which they could not live," which undoubtedly refers to sacrificing infants (v 31). This is an interesting example of the dialogue that took place with popular religion. The author does not entirely deny that there are links between human sacrifices and the worship of Yhwh, but, rather, tries to explain to his listeners that putting these sacrifices into practice is a sign of God's anger.

Genesis 22 at first seems to have a similar aim. This didactic passage explains that the only human sacrifice that is demanded by God applies to this particular context (to test Israel's ancestor); the passage explains that God himself replaced such an offering with animal sacrifice. Genesis 22 then could be read as an incisive polemic against human sacrifice.

But there are other ways the text can be interpreted. During the period of the Babylonian exile, the people of Judah were in a condition of profound despair. Had God forgotten all his promises? Should the people's future be sacrificed on the altar of assimilation into Babylonian culture? So, in Genesis 22, Abraham's experience reflects the situation of the Jewish community exiled in Babylon: deprived of its identity and faced with the prospect of sacrificing its own future. In that way, Genesis 22 prefigures the experience of a God whose plans and purposes are incomprehensible.

At the same time, the Aqedah (the Binding of Isaac) narrative raises the issue of the personal image we have of God: we want a God who corresponds to the ideal of the enlightened human being, a just God, and therefore a God who fits our conception of this enlightened human being. But such a "politically correct" God risks becoming, to use the biblical authors' own words, an idol who does nothing but legitimize merely human aspirations.

Several contemporary Jewish thinkers also see a link between the Aqedah narrative and the Holocaust. The sufferings of the people of Israel under German and European fascism raise the question of how to speak about God after Auschwitz. Has God become extremely cruel, or has he withdrawn from the cruel world of humanity?

The same questions are also present, though in a different way, in the Judges 11 narrative.

The Sacrifice of Jephthah's Daughter

Judges 11:29–40 reads like the "feminine" version of the one we have been examining. In both passages, a father is required to offer his child as a "burnt offering" (Gen 22:2; Judg 11:30); in both cases the child is presented as the "only child" of the father (Gen 22:2; Judg 11:34). The verb *to see* plays an important role in both passages: Abraham tells Isaac that God "will see" the sacrificial victim (Gen 22:8), and Jephthah sees his daughter, who then becomes the intended victim. After the substitution of a ram for Isaac, God promises Abraham innumerable descendants (Gen 22:17), while Jephthah's daughter will disappear without having slept with a man (Judg 11:39). And the "happy ending" in Genesis 22 becomes a tragic ending.

The author of Judges 11 apparently knew the story of Genesis 22. That means that the narrative in Judges 11:29 is not a residue from archaic times when Israel had not yet attained a high degree of spirituality, as asserted by several commentators. On the contrary, we are dealing with a text that had been inserted afterward into the historiographical works of the exilic period from Deuteronomy to 2 Kings. But why insert something around the fifth or fourth century BC?

Let us look at the difference in construction between Judges 11 and Genesis 22. In the story of the sacrifice of Jephthah's anonymous daughter, God does not order it to happen. It is Jephthah himself who, when he finds himself at war against the Ammonites, makes a vow to God: "If you will give the Ammonites into my hand, then whoever comes out of the doors of my house [first] to meet me, when I return victorious from the Ammonites, shall be the LORD's, to be offered up by me as a burnt offering" (Judg 12:30–31). The tragic consequence of the vow is this: it is his daughter who rushes out to welcome her father and who is then chosen for the sacrifice.

The following text shows how the story of Jephthah's daughter was added afterward to the Deuteronomistic historiography. In its primitive version, it makes no mention of Jephthah's vow. In fact, Judges 11:29, 32–33, and 12:1–7 form a narrative unity that contains no mention of Jephthah's daughter.

INSERTION OF "JEPHTHAH'S DAUGHTER" INTO THE DEUTERONOMISTIC HISTORY

The interpolations of the story of Jephthah's daughter are in italics:

Then the spirit of the LORD came upon Jephthah, and he passed through Gilead and Manasseh. He passed on to Mizpah of Gilead, and from Mizpah of Gilead he passed on to the Ammonites.

And Jephthah made a vow to the LORD, and said, "If you will give the Ammonites into my hand, then whoever comes out of the doors of my house [first] to meet me, when I return victorious from the Ammonites, shall be the LORD's, to be offered up by me as a burnt offering."

So Jephthah crossed over to the Ammonites to fight against them; and the LORD gave them into his hand. He inflicted a massive defeat on them from Aroer to the neighborhood of Minnith, twenty towns, and as far as Abel-keramim. So the Ammonites were subdued before the people of Israel.

Then Jephthah came to his home at Mizpah; and there was his daughter coming out to meet him with timbrels and with dancing. She was his only child; he had no son or daughter except her. When he saw her, he tore his clothes, and said, "Alas, my daughter! You have brought me very low; you have become the cause of great trouble to me. For I have opened my mouth to the LORD, and I cannot take back my vow." She said to him, "My father, if you have opened your mouth to the LORD, do to me according to what has gone out of your mouth, now that the LORD has given you vengeance against your enemies, the Ammonites." And she said to her father, "Let this thing be done for me: Grant me two months, so that I may go and wander on the mountains, and bewail my virginity, my companions and I." "Go," he said and sent her away for two months. So she departed, she and her companions, and bewailed her virginity on the mountains. At the end of two months, she returned to her father, who did with her according to the vow he had made. She had never slept with a man. So there arose an Israelite custom that for four days every year the daughters of Israel would go out to lament the daughter of Jephthah the Gileadite.

The men of Ephraim were called to arms, and they crossed to Zaphon and said to Jephthah, "Why did you cross over to fight against the Ammonites, and did not call us to go with you? We will burn your house down over you!"

Jephthah said to them, "My people and I were engaged in conflict with the Ammonites who oppressed us severely. But when I called you, you did not deliver me from their hand. When I saw that you would not deliver me, I took my life in my hand, and crossed over against the Ammonites, and the LORD gave them into my hand. Why then have you come up to me this day, to fight against me?" Then Jephthah gathered all the men of Gilead and fought with Ephraim; and the men of Gilead defeated Ephraim, because they said, "You are fugitives from Ephraim, you Gileadites—in the heart of Ephraim and Manasseh." (Judg 11:29—12:4)

A parallel immediately comes to mind when reading the narrative of Jephthah's daughter's tragic sacrifice: the story of Iphigenia as presented to us by the ancient Athenian playwright Euripides (480–406 BC). In the play *Iphigenia in Tauris*, King Agamemnon—in the throes of military crisis—promises the goddess that he will sacrifice to her the best of whatever the year will bring to him, and the oracle chooses his daughter. Jephthah and Agamemnon each has the same ambiguous reaction when faced with the sacrifice: each feels sorry for himself and blames his daughter for his obligation to sacrifice her because she came out to greet them. In Judges 11, as in Euripides, the true heroes of the tale are the daughters who accept death in order to fulfill their father's vow. Apparently, the author of Judges 11 wishes to present Jephthah's daughter as a kind of Hebrew Iphigenia. This story can be explained by the growing influence that Hellenistic culture had on Judaism from the fifth century BC on. During this period, Hellenism just like Judaism was going through a "theological crisis" regarding the intervention of the gods in the lives of human beings. We might consider the attitude of God in Judges 11 shocking. He apparently accepts Jephthah's vow since the military campaign succeeds, and then does not intervene to oppose a human sacrifice. In fact, God does not intervene at all in this narrative. A cruel God who tolerates the burning of human beings in his name? Some theologians have complained that God takes Jephthah's part against his daughter. Such a modern (and comprehensible) critique hardly does justice to the text. God's silence in this story denounces the attempt of human beings who want to justify foolish or inhuman projects by appealing to God.

Jephthah's thoughtless and irresponsible vow has fatal consequences. The narrator who passes on this miniature tragedy to us could be a contemporary of Ecclesiastes (Qoheleth), who states: "When you make a vow to God, do not delay fulfilling it; for he has no pleasure in fools. Fulfill what you vow. It is better that you should not vow than that you should vow and not fulfill it" (Eccl 5:4–5).

We find ourselves confronted with a certain theological skepticism regarding the idea that the various actions human beings take in order to worship God (including vows) can guarantee contact with God, "for God is in heaven, and you upon earth." This maxim of Ecclesiastes (5:2) applies quite aptly to the spirit of Judges 11. The author of Judges 11 also distances himself from the idea that God was trying to test or to educate Abraham in Genesis 22. He depicts a God who can seem cruel to us, but who proves to be primarily a God who is silent in the face of human aberrations and who confronts human beings with their own cruelty.

The two episodes that we have looked at present a distant God that is impossible for the believer to come to know. But there are other passages in which God is seen to be close to human beings, but for the purpose of eliminating them.[8]

A GOD WHO COMES TO KILL

Jacob and Moses are two figures who are of prime importance for building the Jewish identity. Jacob is the ancestor of the twelve tribes—which according to the Biblical narrative constitute the people of Israel. Moses is the one who brings the Torah from God to the Israelite people, and is the mediator between the people and its God. Interestingly, these two figures, both chosen by God, will have experiences in which they encounter God as an adversary, a dangerous force who comes to kill them, or at least to do them harm.

Jacob's Dangerous Encounter with God

For Jacob, the experience takes place during a time of crisis; he must cross the ford of the Jabbok to confront his brother Esau, with whom he had seriously quarreled at an earlier time in his life. Since his last meeting with Esau, Jacob has become prosperous; he has formed his clan and established his independence from his father-in-law, Laban. All that remains is for him to return home, and it is just at that moment that everything is jeopardized by an unexpected attack during the night, when divine aggression intervenes and threatens Jacob.

> The same night he got up and took his two wives, his two maids, and his eleven children, and crossed the ford of the Jabbok. He took them and sent them across the stream, and likewise everything that he had. Jacob was left alone; and a man

wrestled with him until daybreak. When the man saw that he did not prevail against Jacob, he struck him on the hip socket; and Jacob's hip was put out of joint as he wrestled with him. Then he said, "Let me go, for the day is breaking." But Jacob said, "I will not let you go, unless you bless me." So he said to him, "What is your name?" And he said, "Jacob." Then the man said, "You shall no longer be called Jacob, but Israel, for you have striven with God and with humans, and have prevailed." Then Jacob asked him, "Please tell me your name." But he said, "Why is it that you ask my name?" And there he blessed him. So Jacob called the place Peniel, saying, "For I have seen God face to face, and yet my life is preserved." The sun rose upon him as he passed Penuel, limping because of his hip. (Gen 32:23–32)

Moses' Dangerous Encounter with God

As for the attack against Moses, it comes at the end of the long narrative of his calling, where Yhwh reveals himself as the one who is with Moses and his people (Exod 3:1–22). Next, all the objections that Moses raises in order to be discharged from his mission are decisively pushed aside by God (4:1–18). The reader can at last breathe a huge sigh of relief: the freedom that had been promised is about to be realized. But at that precise moment, everything is shaken up, and in a more brutal way than ever before. God wants to kill the prophet and liberator whom he himself had appointed.

On the way [back to Egypt], at a place where they spent the night, the LORD met him and tried to kill him. But Zipporah took a flint and cut off her son's foreskin, and touched Moses' feet[9] with it, and said, "Truly you are a bridegroom [or kinsman][10] of blood to me!" So he let him alone. It was then she said, "A bridegroom of blood by circumcision." (Exod 4:24–26)

The parallels between this passage and Genesis 32:23–32 are obvious:

- The two narratives lead to a transformation of the hero: the changing of Jacob's status is marked by his name (Jacob becomes Israel), just as that of Moses is marked by circumcision.
- In both cases the hero is surprised during a journey back to his place of "origin": Jacob to Palestine, Moses to Egypt.
- The two attacks take place during the night.
- In Genesis 32, the attacker touches (*naga'*) Jacob's hip; in Exodus 4, Zipporah touches (*naga'*) Moses' "feet."
- Both attacks are followed by an encounter (the verb *pagash*—"to encounter"—is used in Gen 33:18 and Exod 4:27) with a brother that turns out extremely well: Jacob joyfully encounters his brother Esau; Moses joyfully encounters his brother Aaron. Thus, in both narratives, the fight with God proves to be a prerequisite for a harmonious relationship between human beings.

The author of Exodus 4:24ff is largely inspired by the Genesis 32 narrative, but has made it more radical and "demonic." From the beginning, the aggressor is identified as being Yhwh, whose motive is clearly to kill.[11] It is not surprising that the rabbis and the Fathers of the Church have never been comfortable with this story. As for Jacob, it could be assumed that God wants to correct him for his many frauds; as regards Moses, we could conclude that he had not circumcised his son. But the texts themselves give no indication of what fault might have provoked divine aggression. Modern exegetes have suggested that the passages in question are archaic remnants. The deity that appears in them is a demonic entity that has its roots in pagan superstition and is not the God of the Hebrew people. In reality, this argument does not solve anything. Why would the biblical authors identify a demonic force with the God of the Hebrew Bible? Moreover, we could just as easily demonstrate that Genesis 32 and Exodus 4:24–26 are texts that come out of a more recent age and do not contain any of these allegedly archaic elements.

As we have already pointed out, the aggression of the deity transforms the two founding figures.

Let us first consider Jacob. The patriarch changes his name: he becomes "Israel," a name that the text explains as "he has fought with God [El]."[12] We could go as far as to say that the passage serves to highlight the etymology of the name of the people identified with that of their ancestor. The changing of the name in a sense reflects the quest for a new identity. The ancestral, tribal name is called into question and replaced by another one, that of the people of God, which has still to be defined.

Moses too changes his status in relation to circumcision. What is particularly remarkable here is the fact that his life is saved from God's attack thanks to the intervention of his wife Zipporah. In Exodus 4:24–26, she is the only human person who has a name, and she is Yhwh's opponent. After Exodus 1:15–22 (Pharaoh's command to kill all newborn Hebrews is thwarted by the Egyptian midwives), and 2:1–10 (Moses is saved by Pharaoh's daughter), here with Zipporah we have the third narrative in the Book of Exodus that is marked by the actions of a woman. Again it is a foreign woman, a Midianite, an "Arab" woman, who is Moses' wife.

During the time of the return from the Babylonian exile, such mixed marriages posed a problem. The Books of Ezra and Nehemiah show that an emerging orthodoxy, accepted by only a fraction of those who had returned from exile, believed that a rigorous ethnic exclusivity was essential to the identity of Judaism. Ezra and Nehemiah, acting on this idea of exclusivity, required that existing marriages between Jews and foreign women be dissolved, and insisted that foreigners be excluded from Jewish feasts such as Passover (Ezra 10; Neh 13:23–27). This strict application of exclusivity rules was not supported by all Judeans.

Exodus 4:24–26 contributes to the debate on this issue by describing how Zipporah, who is a non-Jewish woman, was assimilated into Moses' people, not simply by marriage, but also by blood. In fact, the story shows the transition of Zipporah from being part of her own family to becoming an integral part of Moses' people. It is Zipporah herself who achieves that integration by opposing Yhwh as he sought to kill Moses. Is this the Yhwh of the "fundamentalists" in Jerusalem, those who were advocating ethnic "exclusivity"? Through the symbolic act that she carries out in circumcising her son and putting that blood on Moses' genitals, she is repeating the wedding night, the night of union and intimacy par excellence. The fact that the child had not been circumcised means that mother and son were not yet part of Israel; by the action of the mother, the integration can take place. Zipporah's declaration in verse 25b—"You are a bridegroom of blood to me"—confirms this new relationship. The link that unites a couple is stronger than any sociological, ethnic, or religious considerations.

However, it is not just the integration of the mother and the son. We must not forget that it is Zipporah who saves Moses from the divine attack by circumcising her son. For an "orthodox" reader, the status of Moses could appear equally problematic. The theological problem is as follows: Because Moses is an "Egyptian Jew," he must have been circumcised, but not according to the "orthodox" rite. Is this the reason for Yhwh's attack? The text does not tell us. However, it does highlight that because of the rite performed by Zipporah, Yhwh leaves Moses alone. This rite then functions as a symbolic circumcision, showing the validity of Moses' circumcision.

Again we take note of the astonishing fact that it is a woman who carries out the circumcision and, furthermore, a foreign woman, which means she breaks a double taboo. She carries out an action that ordinarily is reserved for insiders, and she dares to confront the God of Israel. The term for circumcision used to describe what Zipporah did is not the technical term normally used in the Bible, but instead the verb *cut*, which is often used in Hebrew in the expression "to conclude an alliance." In Genesis 17, it is the circumcision that marks out the alliance of God with Abraham. It is therefore extended through the intermediacy of a woman to anyone who wishes to belong to the people of Yhwh.

The two passages, Genesis 32 and Exodus 4, are part of the great national epics of the Hebrew people: the patriarchal epic and the epic of the exodus from Egypt. There is always a risk that these original stories can be read and interpreted in a triumphalist way. The events suffered by Jacob and Moses at God's hands also countered the arguments of fundamentalists who believe they know the truth about God and mankind.

However, there remains the fact that God's behavior seems cruel and defies explanation. It is incomprehensible and scandalous that Yhwh should want to kill someone whom he has called into his service. We should not offer quick, and somewhat trivial, explanations of this, for example: "It is not extraordinary, biblically speaking, that God would attack his servant. It is a manifestation of His jealous love."[13] On the contrary, behind these verses is the experience of the reformer Martin Luther that he called *deus absconditus*, the "hidden God," which we find in several Old Testament writings from the Persian period, and particularly in the Book of Job.

In discussing theology, we must resist the temptation to deny the inexplicable side of the God of the Bible. The texts that we have just commented on make that quite plain. Similarly, Christianity is unthinkable without the scandal of the cross: "My God, my God, why have you abandoned me?" The Psalmist's cry in the mouth of Jesus about to die on the cross is something that takes us beyond the limits of reasoned theological discussion.

GOD'S CRUELTY OR HUMANITY'S?

Is God cruel? Does he behave like an adversary to human beings? The four stories we have been considering are stories that come out of cruel or fatal human practices: fundamentalist tendencies, infant sacrifices. And divine behavior that today we might find cruel is the sort of behavior that calls into question the cruelty of human beings. In other words, these texts are really about the cruelty of human beings, not the cruelty of God. We could then ask the question whether the cruelty of God is not simply the cruelty of human beings transferred to God. But that is a psychological and somewhat easy interpretation.

Most of humanity's great religious texts contain passages in which a deity fights against a man, often without any apparent reason. These texts remind humankind of the fragility of its existence but also of its theological concepts. When God appears as a dark or cruel God, the believer can only follow the example of Job. At the very point at which he denounces the cruelty of God with unheard-of audacity, Job has no other recourse but to cry: "I know that my Redeemer lives" (Job 19:25). He cries it to God—indeed, even against God.

CHAPTER 3

IS GOD A
WARLIKE DESPOT?

Gott mit uns ("God with us") was the slogan on German soldiers' belt buckles during the First and Second World Wars.
They were convinced, through their faith in the patriotic
preaching of clergy in both the Protestant and Catholic
Churches, that they were engaged in a just war and one that
was willed by God. Legitimizing wars and exterminating
entire populations have, unfortunately, been constants
throughout the history of Christianity, and there is no need
to give copious examples here. From the Crusades to the
various conflicts that have disturbed the Middle East, the
invocation of a God who is a warlord demanding absolute
submission could easily be based on a number of Old
Testament texts where the theme of God as both warrior and
absolute sovereign plays a major role. It would be dishonest
to trivialize these texts by "spiritualizing" them (as God's
calling Israel to combat idolatry), but it would also be theologically questionable to reject the warrior-God of the Old
Testament in opposition to the God of love of the New
Testament.[1] The warlike and tyrannical conceptions of
God are covered mainly in the Book of Deuteronomy and
the conquest narratives of the Book of Joshua, and in the
books that form part of the historiographical range, from

Deuteronomy to 2 Kings. As previously noted, specialists call this historiographical group Deuteronomist. The origins of Deuteronomist theology lie in the Kingdom of Judah in the seventh century BC. This era is characterized by the Assyrian Empire's domination of the ancient Near East.

Since the reign of Tiglath-Pileser (745–727 BC), the Levant had been part of the Assyrian Empire. The Northern Kingdom of Israel had to pay tribute from the year 738. From 722 (the fall of Samaria), it lost its independence and became an Assyrian province. The king of the Southern Kingdom of Judah became a vassal of the Assyrian king in 734. The small states of Syria-Palestine were then subject to the *pax assyrica*, which was a sort of common market before its time. The creation of a true infrastructure (military and commercial routes, a system of communication between the center and the periphery) brought about mobility that was unparalleled in the history of Mesopotamia. In addition, there were other innovations: the enlistment of soldiers from the annexed countries into the Assyrian army, as well as the deportation of part of the subjugated population. In fact, these deportations were mostly of the intelligentsia (officials, scribes, key military personnel, priests, and elite artisans),[2] which was aimed at preventing the populace from organizing uprisings. These deportees were "replaced" either by Assyrian functionaries, or by other groups of foreigners who were forced to collaborate with the local Assyrian administration. The presence of Assyrian culture and propaganda everywhere caused "culture shock"[3] in Israel and in Judah, as in the neighboring kingdoms, which thus far had been sheltered from great international politics. The Assyrians distributed legal documents and propaganda in which the Assyrian king required the total submission of his vassals and which celebrated Assyrian victories and the extermination of all Assyria's enemies.

The spreading of Assyrian ideology is the first example of the globalization of a dominant culture, and we can say without exaggeration that the encounter that Judean intellectuals had with Assyrian ideology had a profound and decisive effect on the formation of the Old Testament.

In the seventh century BC, Jerusalem experienced a notable economic boom, and its population grew considerably. Here we can see the consequence of the destruction of Samaria by Assyria.[4] The reign of King Josiah (640–609) was probably the culmination of this development. Again, benefiting from a weakening of the Assyrian presence in Palestine, Josiah and his counselors prepared a political and theological "reform." The temple in Jerusalem was declared the only legitimate sanctuary for the worship of Yhwh, and this facilitated the control of the clergy and of taxes. It is during this period of strong nationalism that a first draft of the Book of Deuteronomy was produced. This work accompanied, supported, and justified the changes taking place. As we will see, the influence of Assyrian ideology and style can be easily identified.

YHWH, LIEGE LORD: DEUTERONOMY

"Hear, O Israel: The LORD is our God, the LORD alone. You shall love the LORD your God with all your heart, and with all your soul, and with all your might" (Deut 6:4–5). This appeal, which has become the fundamental confession of faith of Judaism and which is still recited today by believers, constitutes without doubt the heart of the primitive Deuteronomy of the seventh century. Here we will not discuss the significance of "Yhwh alone" (literally: "one Yhwh"), since it has been covered in the Introduction. The statement is addressed to those who venerated Yhwh under many forms, and in many sanctuaries. Deuteronomy insists on the unity of Yhwh; the affirmation is equivalent to saying that he is indivisible and that he requires total adherence from the people who want to worship him. This is the sense in which we should understand verse 5: If Yhwh is indivisible, then love for him must be total and seamless.

But what does "you shall love Yhwh" mean? Can you command love? Any lover will tell you how impossible that is. Apparently, the verb *love* here has a sense that is neither sentimental nor passionate. In fact, in Deuteronomy 10:12, the exhortation to love God is accompanied by verbs like *fear, serve,* and *obey.* These terms belong more to the semantic field of loyalty and submission, and we can find astonishing similarities to this command to love in the Assyrian vassal treaties[5] where the high king must be "loved" by his vassals:

> You shall love Assurbanipal…son of Assarhaddon, king of Assyria, as yourself." (Treaty of Assarhaddon, 672 BC)

> We will love Assurbanipal, king of Assyria, and hate his enemy. From this day and for as long as we live, Assurbanipal will be our king and lord. We will neither establish nor seek another king or lord for ourselves." (Treaty of Assurbanipal, around 650 BC)

The parallels with the central commandment of Deuteronomy are clear: Yhwh is presented in Josiah's reforms like an Assyrian liege lord. We can expand this par-

allel a little further, since the organization of the entire Book
of Deuteronomy could be understood as coming out of the
Assyrian vassal treaties. The following elements of the Book
of Deuteronomy occur in the Assyrian vassal treaties:

- They contain (in most cases) a "historical prologue," narrating the encounter between the
  liege lord and the vassal.
- There is a principal commandment (exclusive
  allegiance to the Assyrian king).
- There are specific stipulations (tribute, military
  obligations, and so on).
- There is an appeal to the gods as witnesses who
  guarantee the validity of the treaty.
- There are blessings and curses for those who do
  or do not respect the stipulations of the treaty.

It is easy to see that all these elements are to be found in
Deuteronomy: the forms of the curses in Deuteronomy
28:20 onward are so like a treaty with Esarhaddon, King of
Assyria, that it can only be explained by a literary dependence. Even the appeal to witnesses is repeated, though in a
roundabout way. Since Yhwh cannot make appeal to other
deities, Deuteronomy 30:19 notes: "I call heaven and earth
to witness against you today."

What conclusion should we draw from the fact that the
authors of Deuteronomy use a vassal treaty as a model to
describe the relationship between Yhwh and his people? In
fact, *berît*, the central term in Deuteronomy, which we translate as *alliance* or *covenant*, could be rendered equally well by
the word *treaty*. Are we then in the presence of an oppressive
theology, where God appears as a tyrant who demands
blind obedience from his faithful servants, and sanctions all
transgressions against his laws by the worst maledictions?

If we put Deuteronomy in the context of Assyrian domination, its message can be summarized thus: Yes, Israel has a liege lord who demands absolute faithfulness. However, this is not the Assyrian high king, but Yhwh, the God of his people. So the use of an Assyrian model could have a subversive anti-Assyrian meaning. Israel must obey only God, and no other.

However, there is still a problem: this God is often depicted in the Deuteronomistic texts as a warrior-God.

YHWH, GOD OF CONQUEST: JOSHUA

The first part of the Book of Joshua (Josh 1–12) explains to the reader that the establishment of the Hebrew people in their own land is brought about by a military conquest where Yhwh appears as a warlord with Joshua as his general. This general leads his people to numerous victories which most often result in the extermination or expulsion of the Canaanite population. Here, Yhwh is clearly presented as a warrior-God who is the high chief of a people who are just as warlike as he is. These are the very texts that are used today in some Jewish fundamentalist circles for opposing the peace process between Israelis and Palestinians and calling for the expulsion of the Arab population, just as they have been used throughout history by fundamentalist Christians, such as Oliver Cromwell, to advocate annihilation of their enemies. This fundamentalist reading of the Book of Joshua is doubly suspect: first, it takes the narratives in Joshua to be historical documents, and second, it completely obscures the fact that the exaltation of a warrior-God poses a huge problem for biblical faith.

As for the aforementioned period, when the Israelite

tribes were establishing themselves in their own land (twelfth/eleventh centuries BC), we now know, thanks mostly to Israeli archaeological work, that the establishment of the clans and tribes that would become Israel came about as a result of a long and complex process, which is very unlike some of the conquest narratives in Joshua.[6] For the most part, Israel evolved out of native Canaanite populations. They came out of marginal groups who were often in conflict with the kings of the Canaanite city-states, which depended on the king of Egypt. These rebel populations are called *Hapiru* or *Habiru* in some Egyptian documents, an expression that has often been linked to the term *Hebrew*. The *Habiru* are attested outside of Canaan, in Egypt also, and this may explain how the formation of Israel was a confederation of these groups. It would have been a group from Egypt that would pass on the experience of being liberated from the Egyptians, thanks to the intervention of Yhwh. Such an experience would naturally have been relevant for the Canaanite *Habiru* who had also suffered under Egyptian power. This historical reconstruction means that a large part of the future Israel would be composed of a native Canaanite population. Consequently, the establishment of the Hebrew people in Canaan did not come about as a result of a blitzkrieg or an invasion led by an external army.

So where does the violent depiction of conquest and extermination in the Book of Joshua come from? Although specialists debate a number of details, there is some consensus over the fact that the first collection of conquest narratives in Joshua 1–12 came into being during the Assyrian era and probably under the reign of King Josiah (around 620 BC). We know that Josiah could have benefited from the weakening of the Assyrian Empire and could have considered a policy of conquest aimed at integrating into the

Kingdom of Judah some of the territories from the ancient Kingdom of the North, which, after 722, had been a province of Assyria. In this context, the Book of Joshua provides a theological legitimization of Josiah's expansion policy. The Deuteronomistic authors who had already written the first version of Deuteronomy give Joshua and Josiah parallel stories and by doing so develop a warlike vision of Israel's origins. By presenting Yhwh as a warrior-God who intervenes in the wars of his people, the Deuteronomists are not demonstrating any originality. Such a militaristic view was already present among the Assyrians and then later among the Babylonians.[7] The authors of Joshua were greatly inspired by Assyrian texts in presenting Yhwh as the God of conquest.

The Book of Joshua opens with a great speech by which God establishes Joshua as a warlord and gives him the following promises: "Every place that the sole of your foot will tread upon I have given to you....No one shall be able to stand against you....Be strong and courageous" (Josh 1:3, 5, 6). There is a similar text from Joshua 10:8, when a decisive battle is about to begin: "Do not fear them, for I have handed them over to you; not one of them shall stand before you." We find the same mixture of exhortation and assurance of victory over enemies in an oracle to the Assyrian ruler Esarhaddon: "Esarhaddon, king of the nations, fear not!...I am Ishtar of Arbela. I will flay your enemies and give them to you....Fear not!"[8]

The narratives of the Assyrian conquest are built according to a stereotyped[9] model, from which the Deuteronomistic authors were mostly inspired to develop an ideology of the "war of Yhwh" (e.g., Deut 20; Josh 10; Judg 4, etc.). Numbers 21:14 also makes reference to a book with this very title. We may note in passing that it is not appropriate here to speak of a "holy war," a mistake that is often made. In the traditional concept of a holy war, it is the people who fight for their God; in Assyrian and Old Testament texts, it is God who fights for his people. The constituent elements of this ideology are the following:

1. The enemy is poised to attack Israel.
2. The reaction of Israel is discouragement, fear, and entreaties to Yhwh.
3. Israel is exhorted not to fear the enemy but to believe in Yhwh.
4. Yhwh goes before Israel and wins the battle.
5. Yhwh's miraculous intervention causes the enemy to be discouraged.
6. This leads to a total victory over the enemy.
7. The enemy is pursued and exterminated.

The Assyrian influences over a text like Joshua 10, for example, are obvious in a letter written by the Assyrian ruler Sargon to his god.[10] Like Sargon, Joshua and Israel must confront an immense coalition of enemy kings. Thanks to divine intervention, the enemy is routed in both cases, and during their flight, Adad and Yhwh intervene in a miraculous way:

> The rest of the people are fleeing for their lives....Adad [the storm God]...uttered a loud cry against them. With the help of torrential rain and rocks from heaven [hail], he annihilated those who remained. (Sargon's "Letter to God")

> As they fled before Israel, while they were going down the slope of Beth-horon, the LORD threw down huge stones from heaven on them as far as

> Azekah, and they died; there were more who died
> because of the hailstones than the Israelites killed
> with the sword. (Josh 10:11)

In using the Assyrian model for the conquest, the authors of Joshua 1–12 have highlighted the warlike image of Yhwh, of a God who does not hesitate to radically exterminate all of Israel's enemies. Such an emphasis is regrettable. Nevertheless, we must understand it in the historical context in which it appears, because the authors of Joshua are pursuing a polemical aim, similar to that of the authors of the Book of Deuteronomy. For the authors of the time of King Josiah, the aim is to show that Yhwh is stronger than Assur, Hadad, or Ishtar, the tutelary gods of Assyria. When the Book of Joshua insists on the fact that other peoples have no right to occupy Canaan, this applies equally, and predominantly, to the Assyrians who in the seventh century were occupying the land promised by God to his people. The term *counter-history* can be applied here (an expression that comes from within Jewish studies): an oppressed minority group takes up the oppressor's own argument in order to ridicule it or turn it against the oppressor. There is, therefore, a polemical message in the Book of Joshua affirming the superiority of Yhwh over Assyria and its gods, but the message is developed at the expense of making Yhwh appear as severe and warlike as Assur.

"DISARMING" THE GOD OF CONQUEST

We cannot deny the power of the image of a warlike God in the Hebrew Bible. However, we must also highlight the fact that this image is counterbalanced by other passages that modify or critique it. When Jerusalem was destroyed by Babylonian troops in 587 BC, the concept of a national warlike God was profoundly shaken. So the introduction to the Book of Joshua was revised and corrected by the second- or third-generation Deuteronomists. The military speech addressed to Joshua turns into a sermon on the Law, and Joshua passes from the status of a military leader to that of a conscientious rabbi, as is evident in Joshua 1:8: "This book of the law shall not depart out of your mouth; you shall meditate on it day and night." So it is respect for the Torah, and no longer for military exploits, that is the deciding factor in the lives of the people in the land.

A similar "demilitarization" occurs in the first version of the miracle of the parting of the Red Sea in Exodus 14. For a very long time, it has been recognized that the central passage in Exodus 14 is composed of two different versions: a priestly version and another that we could call Deuteronomistic, since those authors seem to belong to the intellectual descendants of the Deuteronomists. This version— which undoubtedly emerged at the beginning of the Persian era—resumes the ideology of the war of Yhwh. However, a demilitarization of this concept can also be observed. What is particularly remarkable in the Exodus passage is the exhortation to Israel to keep still. It is Yhwh alone who fights. Israel has nothing to do other than see and believe: "The LORD will fight for you, and you have only to keep still" (Exod 14:14).

The author of the Deuteronomistic version of Exodus 14 stresses the power of Yhwh in a crisis situation where that power was clearly challenged. In fact, this text presupposes the experience of the Babylonian exile where the deportees must have felt crushed by Babylonian culture, power, and splendor. Therefore, this passage is aimed at an audience that has been deprived of all political and military power and is completely incapable of bringing about its own deliverance. Exodus 14 shows, then, that liberation comes from no one but Yhwh. At the same time, this passage calls into question the historicity of the war as a strictly human occurrence. The human war is based on and subsumed into the liberating action of God. It is scarcely an exaggeration to say that the theology of Yhwh's war, in the form we find it in this text and also in the exilic passages from the Book of Joshua, is no longer based on an ideological warlike framework, but can be understood in the context of a kind of "liberation theology."

Exodus 13 and 14:
The Deuteronomistic Version

Chapter 13: When Pharaoh let the people go....The LORD went in front of them in a pillar of cloud by day, to lead them along the way, and in a pillar of fire by night, to give them light, so that they might travel by day and by night. Neither the pillar of cloud by day nor the pillar of fire by night left its place in front of the people. (Exod 13:17, 21–22)

Chapter 14: When the king of Egypt was told that the people had fled, the minds of Pharaoh and his officials were changed toward the people, and they said, "What have we done, letting Israel leave our service?" So he had his chariot made ready, and took his army with him....The Egyptians pursued them, all Pharaoh's horses and chariots, his chariot drivers and his army; they overtook them camped by the sea....

In great fear the Israelites cried out to the LORD....But Moses said to the people, "Do not be afraid, stand firm, and see the deliverance that the LORD will accomplish for you today; for the Egyptians whom you see today you shall never see again. The LORD will fight for you, and you have only to keep still."

...It [the cloud] came between the army of Egypt and the army of Israel. And so the cloud...lit up the night; one did not come near the other all night.

...The LORD drove the sea back by a strong east wind all night, and turned the sea into dry land; and the waters were divided....At the morning watch the LORD in the pillar of fire and cloud looked down upon the Egyptian army, and threw the Egyptian army into panic. He clogged their chariot wheels so that they turned with difficulty. The Egyptians said, "Let us flee from the Israelites, for the LORD is fighting for them against Egypt."

...At dawn the sea returned to its normal depth. As the Egyptians fled before it, the LORD tossed the Egyptians into the sea. The waters returned and covered the chariots and the chariot drivers, the entire army of Pharaoh that had followed them into the sea; not one of them remained....

Thus the LORD saved Israel that day from the Egyptians; and Israel saw the Egyptians dead on the seashore. Israel saw the great work that the Lord did against the Egyptians. So the people feared the LORD. (Exod 14:5, 6, 9b, 10b, 13–14, 20, 21b, 24–25, 27b, 30)

A similar demilitarization of warlike traditions appears in First and Second Chronicles. These books, which date from the beginning of the Hellenistic period, provide a reinterpretation of the history of Israel as it appears from the Book of Genesis to First and Second Kings. In this revision, all the references to the military conquest of the country are omitted! We pass directly from the genealogical lists presenting the different families descended from the sons of Jacob (1 Chr 1–9) to the establishment of the monarchy (1 Chr 10). As biblical scholar Sara Japhet has highlighted it, Chronicles 1 and 2 present a native Israel that has always been in the land and that does not need a warrior-God to explain how it came to be established in Canaan.[11]

Similarly, the Chronicler transforms the image of the war as it appears in the books of Kings. The kings become liturgical leaders and the wars become a procession. Thus, the famous exegete Julius Wellhausen exclaimed:

> See what Chronicles has made out of David!… The hero at the head of his companions in arms has become the singer and master of ceremonies at the head of a swarm of priests and Levites; his clearly cut figure has become a feeble holy picture, seen through a cloud of incense.[12]

This statement, which Wellhausen intended to be pejorative, has nevertheless an element of truth about it. The kings are no longer primarily executors of the warrior-God's plans, but rather presiders over the celebration of God through worship and psalms. If there is a war, the people are not called upon to fight, but—as is made clear in Exodus 14—they are to be merely spectators of the military exploits of Yhwh. When Judah is threatened by her neighbors, a prophet exhorts King Jehoshaphat and the people saying: "Do not fear or be dismayed...for the battle is not yours but God's. This battle is not for you to fight; take your position, stand still, and see the victory of the LORD on your behalf" (2 Chr 20:15–17).

In a manner of speaking, the war is stolen away from the people. The image of warlike Yhwh no longer serves to justify human war, but to express a hope in the salutary intervention of God on behalf of his people. A similar approach is found in the apocalyptic literature (for example, the second part of the Book of Daniel), which attempts to describe the events preceding the end of the world and often employs warlike metaphors. On the last day, God will intervene to annihilate the forces of evil that oppose him and his people.

This concept will be taken up again by the community of Qumran in a writing that is called the "scroll of war"; it will also influence the New Testament. The last book of the New Testament, the Revelation to St. John, portrays a war-rior-God who protects his people through his actions: "From his mouth comes a sharp sword with which to strike down the nations, and he will rule them with a rod of iron; he will tread the wine press of the fury of the wrath of God the Almighty" (Rev 19:15). Thus, the image of the warrior-God is present in the apocalyptic literature of both the Old as well as the New Testament. It is a mistake to try to set up the two Testaments against each other at this level.

It is undeniable that passages in which God intervenes in wartime play an important part in the Bible. This is not really surprising, given the presence of war throughout the whole of human history. However, we should no more resign ourselves to the Bible's depiction of a warlike God than we should reject en bloc what the Bible has to say about God. As we have seen, biblical passages describing a warlike God were revised during the exile to present a God who was decidedly less violent. These revisions should have made it impossible for human beings to condone, on a biblical basis, war and conquest. Unfortunately, that has not been the case, and the Book of Joshua has been used to justify the extermination of Native Americans and the superiority of white settlers in South Africa, and other injustices. The only weapon that can be used against such abuses of biblical texts is a serious study of the texts themselves, one that takes into account the complexity of how they were passed on. In this regard, we can remind ourselves that the first part of the Hebrew Bible, the Torah or Pentateuch, which constitutes the central part of the Bible for Judaism, intentionally does not include the Book of Joshua and its violent conquest narratives. From the perspective of the story or narrative, this seems odd because the Pentateuch ends with Moses dying before he can enter the promised land—a somewhat "unresolved" ending. Thus, it is no surprise that exegetes have often attempted to attach the Book of Joshua to the Pentateuch, creating a longer, more "complete" narrative called the Hexateuch. However, Judaism has chosen to give the Pentateuch an "open ending" and to relegate the narratives of conquest to a secondary position.

This does not mean that there are no references to a warrior-God in the Pentateuch. It is principally in Deuteronomy that we find texts that seem to present a God of ethnic cleansing, and we cannot ignore these texts.

A GOD OF ETHNIC CLEANSING?

Deuteronomy 7 opens with the following commandment:

> When the LORD your God brings you into the land that you are about to enter and occupy, and he

clears away many nations before you—the Hittites, the Girgashites, the Amorites, the Canaanites, the Perizzites, the Hivites, and the Jebusites, seven nations mightier and more numerous than you— and when the LORD your God gives them over to you and you defeat them, then you must utterly destroy them. Make no covenant with them and show them no mercy. Do not intermarry with them, giving your daughters to their sons or taking their daughters for your sons, for that would turn away your children from following me, to serve other gods. Then the anger of the LORD would be kindled against you, and he would destroy you quickly. But this is how you must deal with them: break down their altars, smash their pillars, hew down their sacred poles, and burn their idols with fire. For you are a people holy to the LORD your God; the LORD your God has chosen you out of all the peoples on earth to be his people, his treasured possession. (7:1–6)

If we think of the dramas that have played out in these last decades of our planet's history, this text is enough to send shivers down the spine. Israel is exhorted to separate itself completely from other peoples, and that separation apparently implies massacring them.[13] We would have a hard time supporting such a text. But let us at least try to understand it. First, it is an ideological commandment that was never applied to the Old Testament times (but unfortunately was, thereafter, by Christians who waged war against heretics). The issue is the identity of Israel and the exclusive worship of Yhwh that is required of it. In fact, the text builds a very strong opposition between Yhwh, the God of Israel, and the gods of "the peoples." The authors of this text, probably from the fifth century BC, were afraid that Israel might lose its identity by entering into contact with "others." Therefore, they adopt a very defensive posture, which, unsurprisingly, comes out in very aggressive language. This violent expression reveals a community in crisis, which feels threatened from all quarters. This attitude can be found even today. Once a society undergoes an economic or ideological crisis, it seeks to close in on itself by advocating the expulsion of foreigners. Passages like Deuteronomy 7 show us that Israel has not always escaped that danger. We can also point out that the list of seven nations in verse 1 does not define particular peoples. First, the number 7 symbolizes totality; also, most of the names, such as Hittites, Amorites, Canaanites, and so on, are general terms that the Assyrians and Babylonians used to describe the entire population of the Levant. Deuteronomy 7 is, therefore, not intended as a list of specific foreigners; the names used have a symbolic value, representing all those who could turn Israel from the exclusive worship of Yhwh. We could go further and remember that when the exiles return, a lively debate arises between some of them and the "indigenous" population who had not been deported. The hardline fringe of exiles think of themselves as the only "true" Israel and group the non-exiles together with the foreigners.

Ezra and Nehemiah want to spread this exclusivist vision of Israel by forbidding any mixing between exiles and non-exiles. Ezra 9 uses a list of peoples similar to the one in Deuteronomy 7 to characterize the "people of the land." Ezra 9:12 defines the prohibition against mixed marriages using almost the same terms as Deuteronomy 7:3[14] (on this point, also see the above comments on Exodus 4, about Moses marrying an outsider). We could conclude that the text of Deuteronomy 7 is attempting to promote a very narrow vision of the people of Yhwh that excludes a large part of the former inhabitants of the Kingdom of Judah. This segregationist view comes out in comments of a violent nature; it can certainly be understood to come from a situation of foreign domination in which Judaism was at risk of being assimilated into the surrounding culture. However, this attitude of withdrawing into itself is not viable. The Hebrew Bible gives us a number of narratives that contrast with this segregationist vision of God, and that seem to underpin some of the texts from the Deuteronomistic tradition.

In the Old Testament, the chronicle of the Hebrew people opens with the history of the patriarchs, which begins with the cycle of Abraham. In contrast to the texts from Deuteronomy and the historical books, we can see in the patriarchal narratives a peaceful or even pacifist approach to the confrontation with the neighboring peoples. Again, Wellhausen observed that the patriarchs show little taste for war. In the Book of Genesis, Israel gives an entirely different image of itself in the midst of the nations.[15] The other peoples are not criticized, there is no mention of their idolatry, and they themselves can maintain an intimate relationship with the God of Israel. Thus Hagar, ancestress of the Arab tribes, will encounter in the desert a messenger of Yhwh who will intervene in her favor. Hagar herself will have the unheard of privilege of contemplating God; at least, that is what the original version of Genesis 16:13 suggests, although as it stands, the verse is somewhat obscure. In this verse, Hagar exclaims, "Have I really seen God and remained alive after seeing him?" So we can see that God (who, in Genesis, is often called El) can be invoked without difficulty by representatives of other peoples, as is the case, for example, with King Abimelek (Gen 20). Thus, in the Book of Genesis, God appears as a "God of coexistence," who certainly chooses Abraham, but does not demand that he separate himself from the other inhabitants of Canaan. The story of Abraham, therefore, could be read as a reaction against a vision that was too nationalistic. The cycle of Abraham shows how the ancestor of the people created a place among the neighboring people without being overridden and without possessing the land exclusively. The God of Abraham is a peaceful God who wants the various peoples to get along together. It is not by chance that the history of the Hebrew people begins by presenting us with a peaceful image of God that counterbalances other biblical images of God as a conqueror.

A similar view can be found in the story of Joseph, which concludes the first book of the Bible (Gen 37–50). This story tells of the adventures and the success of one of Jacob's sons, who was sold into slavery in Egypt by his brothers and presents a Judaism that is more liberal than the orthodox religion of Jerusalem, or even Babylon. The narrative develops a universal theology, and prefers the name *Elohim* rather than Yhwh. There is no emphasis on the particularity of the Yahwistic faith as something that is only for the Hebrew people; on the contrary, Pharaoh and Joseph can conduct theological discussions without encountering problems of any kind. Joseph also has a gift of divination like the high functionaries of Pharaoh's court. In the tradition of Exodus, Egypt is seen as the land of oppression, but in the story of Joseph it is seen as a host country where one can live and even pursue a career, since Joseph becomes Pharaoh's chancellor and the son-in-law of an Egyptian high priest. The Hebrews and Egyptians also practice "mixed marriages," against which first the Deuteronomistic tradition and then Ezra fight so fiercely. So Joseph becomes the ancestor of a Judaism of the Diaspora that seeks integration and a peaceful life in the host country. This story, which reflects a thorough knowledge of Egyptian customs in the second half of the first millennium BC, was originally drafted as a stand-alone narrative. It is even more remarkable that later editors of the Pentateuch included it in the Torah by applying some modifications (mainly reinforcing the role of Judah to stress the necessary link between Judea and the Diaspora). By doing this, a different voice than the mainstream can be discerned in the Torah.

Let us return again to the militaristic Book of Joshua. The chronology of Joshua 1:10 (the announcement regarding the crossing of the Jordan in three days' time) and Joshua 3:2 (the beginning of the crossing of the Jordan after three days) is interrupted in the text by the account of the two spies being sent to the house of Rahab the prostitute, which was apparently inserted afterward to modify the ideology of the conquest. In this story, we can see that it is a Canaanite woman, and one of questionable profession, who saves the Israelite spies whose lives are in danger. It is Rahab who confesses Yhwh as God of heaven and earth and who confirms that Yhwh has given the land to Israel (2:7–11). When the spies return, without having spied out the land at all, they are content, in fact, to relay Rahab's words to Joshua (2:24). Without Rahab, Israel would never have taken possession of the land. Thus, the story of Rahab disrupts and challenges the self-centered and violent account of the origins of Israel, by showing that without the contribution of foreigners, the promise would never have been realized.

YHWH–BETWEEN MILITARISM AND PACIFISM

In the course of our overview of the presentation of Yhwh as a warrior-God, we have stressed the importance of this concept to the Assyrian period. Presenting Yhwh as an Assyrian overlord (in Deuteronomy) or as a powerful and violent Assyrian-style god (in the Book of Joshua) had a partially subversive aim: by claiming for themselves the ideology of the great Assyrian Empire and applying it to Yhwh, the Deuteronomistic authors wanted to show the superiority of the God of Israel in the face of the Assyrian threat. But it was also dangerous for Yhwh to bear the same characteristics as the Assyrian gods. The portrayal of a warrior-God in the conquest narratives has unfortunately been used to legitimize all sorts of atrocities throughout Christian history.

We cannot deny the presence of warlike texts in the Bible. But we must insist on the fact that the warrior-God is never a unilateral or exclusive reference. The epic of the Hebrew people, in fact, opens with the image of an anti-militarist and universal God, and the Hebrew Bible closes by invoking—in First and Second Chronicles—the same universal God who is the God of both the Persian kings and the Jewish people (2 Chr 36:21), a God who promises a future of peace around the rebuilding of the temple.

CHAPTER 4

IS GOD SELF-RIGHTEOUS AND HUMANS MERE SINNERS?

For many contemporary supporters of individual freedom, the God of the Old Testament often appears as a sanctimonious God who issues a whole host of laws that human beings find impossible to keep. These laws, which come together in the Pentateuch, are considered restrictive and oppressive; their aim seems to be to make humanity understand that it has always been in a sinful state. Those who argue in this way against the Old Testament are proposing, without realizing it, a New Testament reading of the Hebrew Bible. They are reinforcing the idea that human beings have been sinners from the beginning, and that they were born sinners because of the fault of the first human couple. But does this idea of original sin, an idea that Paul develops (see Rom 5:12–21; 7:13–23), actually exist in the Hebrew Bible?

THE ACCOUNT OF THE FALL IN GENESIS 3

We often read "the story of the apple" (actually the Hebrew text does not state what fruit it was) in order to demonstrate human beings' incapacity to respect the divine law. We also like to note that misfortune comes into the world through the actions of a woman, as in the Greek myth of Pandora. After the creation of the first couple—first Adam, and then the woman from the man's side (or Adam's face, depending on how the passage is translated)—the couple lives within the divine garden, in the wild. Both of them are naked, but they do not realize it. Only one prohibition is stipulated by Yhwh: "You may freely eat of every tree of the garden; but of the tree of the knowledge of good and evil you shall not eat, for in the day that you eat of it you shall die" (Gen 2:16–17). The ban was disobeyed because of the intervention of the serpent who plays the role of agent provocateur:

> Now the serpent was more crafty than any other wild animal that the LORD God had made. He said to the woman, "Did God say, 'You shall not eat from any tree in the garden'?" The woman said to the serpent, "We may eat of the fruit of the trees in the garden; but God said, 'You shall not eat of the fruit of the tree that is in the middle of the garden, nor shall you touch it, or you shall die.'" But the serpent said to the woman, "You will not die; for God knows that when you eat of it your eyes will be opened, and you will be like God, knowing good and evil." So when the woman saw that the tree was good for food, and that it was a delight to the eyes, and that the tree was to be desired to make one wise, she took of its fruit and ate; and she also gave some to her husband, who was with her, and he ate. Then the eyes of both were opened, and they knew that they were naked. (Gen 3:1–7)

The serpent asserts that the man and the woman will not die, contrary to what God had declared, but instead would become like gods. Who is right? God or the serpent? The answer is a difficult one: the man and the woman do not die immediately as God had said ("the day on which you eat of it, you will die"); and, in fact, they do acquire a knowledge they had lacked, but that knowledge concerned their nakedness. They discover through it that their sexuality is different from that of the animals. The same motif turns up in the ancient Mesopotamian *Epic of Gilgamesh*,[1] when Enkidu, Gilgamesh's "wild-man" opponent (and later friend), sleeps with a prostitute and realizes that he is different from the animals with whom he has been living up until that point. In both accounts, it is the difference between themselves and animals that human beings are first made aware of. They come to understand that their humanity, with a sexuality all their own, is different from that of animals. In this way, they are freed from the cycles of natural reproduction. Therefore, the transgression in Genesis 3 is first of all the discovery of sexuality.

But is it necessary to associate sexuality with sin, as has constantly been the case throughout the history of the Church? In order to be able to respond, we must first examine the role of the serpent. In the narrative, the serpent is certainly not the devil, as the Fathers of the Church and other commentators have claimed. The text states that the serpent is one of God's creatures, the most cunning certainly, but still a creature. One might suspect then that the serpent is, in fact, obeying God's orders. The serpent is an important and ambiguous animal in many mythologies. For the ancients, it is associated with immortality since it molts and therefore appears to invert the aging process.

After the first couple's transgression, Yhwh punishes each of the actors in the drama. The divine sanctions remind readers of the passage of their own realities, as they see and understand them:

- The serpent is condemned to crawl on the ground. This explains the fact that it has no legs, and highlights the danger this animal poses to those working the soil in agricultural Palestine.
- The woman is condemned to bear children in pain and to be submissive to the man.
- Adam is condemned to a soil that's been cursed. His survival will not be guaranteed and will be linked to a life of hard labor.

The text is, therefore, an account of the beginning of things and explains how suffering and death came to be, even if life is still possible. It is only after the sanction that the woman receives a new name, *Hawwa*—Eve; the living one.

In the end, Yhwh expels the man and the woman from the garden, after clothing them in garments. He justifies this expulsion in the following way: "Then the LORD God said, 'See, the man has become like one of us, knowing good and evil; and now, he might reach out his hand and take also from the tree of life, and eat, and live forever'" (Gen 3:22). Here we can note the plural used by God, where, similar to the first account of Creation (Gen 1), he is referring to the celestial court. Hence the need to create a second distinction, between human beings and the divine: this will be Adam's condemnation to a mortal life, by being deprived of eternal life.

Could the man and the woman have resisted the temptation of the serpent and remained forever in the garden? If we read the passage closely, it is doubtful. First, it is surprising that Yhwh, in placing the prohibition, did not already foresee the transgression. He promised nothing in connection with obedience to the commandment as is traditionally the case in the pedagogy of the ancient Near East: blessings for behaving appropriately and curses to guard against disloyal behavior (see the blessings and curses in Deuteronomy 28). The fact that only the transgression is mentioned is therefore significant. It is as if Yhwh wanted to drive the human couple to transgress. Shocking as it may seem at first, this seems to be a useful way to understand the narrative in Genesis 3. In fact, it is a reflection on the freedom of humanity. According to biblical anthropology, a human being is not a robot or a marionette, but an independent, free being, even with respect to God. This freedom allows human beings to sin against God's commandments. Also, in order to become truly human, the human being needs to be separated from God. Human beings cannot live with him, but must leave the garden to live in a place they can call their own. God himself urges human beings to take possession of their freedom by transgressing his commandment. Therefore, this freedom is not absolute because God in some way "manipulates" the situation. Through this complex narrative, the author addresses a great philosophical and theological problem that will be debated throughout the centuries, that of free will. Up to what point is the human being a free, absolute master of his destiny, and in what way does his freedom depend on God?

The same problem arises in the account of the plagues of Egypt in the Book of Exodus (Exod 7–12). In some passages, the king of Egypt refuses to let the Hebrews go despite the manifestations of the power of the God of Israel: "But Pharaoh hardened his heart this time also, and would not let the people go" (Exod 8:32). The plagues appear to be punishment inflicted on a disobedient monarch who causes them through his own obstinate behavior. Therefore, Pharaoh is responsible for what happens to him. However, in other passages the narrator tells us that it is Yhwh himself who hardens Pharaoh's heart, so that he would keep the Israelites in Egypt: "But the LORD hardened the heart of Pharaoh, and he would not listen to them, just as the LORD had spoken to Moses" (Exod 9:12). The two concepts appear contradictory, and exegetes have, with good reason, attributed them to two different authors. However, merging the two approaches together into one story makes sense. It shows that human beings are free and are responsible for their acts and the consequences that result from them; yet at the same time it shows that, nevertheless, it is God who remains the master of human history and who is established over even the most powerful of men (as was the king of Egypt during certain periods).

Returning to Genesis 3, we can see that the story of the fall has nothing to do with original sin, as has often been understood in Christianity. (Indeed, the word *sin* does not appear anywhere in the story; it is first used in Genesis 4 in connection with the first human murder, which we will touch upon in the next chapter.) The story of the fall is a narrative that reflects on the freedom and independence of human beings, and on those characteristics that distinguish human beings from both animals and God. Human beings are distinguished from the animals by a sexuality that is not limited solely to reproduction. They are distinguished from God through their mortal state, which they share with the animals. The expulsion from the garden, although painful, is necessary for human beings to become truly themselves.

A LEGALISTIC GOD?

In order to live in community, human beings need rules. It is not surprising, then, that the core of the Pentateuch contains many important laws and instructions. Rabbinical tradition lists 613 laws or instructions that God ordained for his people through his intermediary Moses. The Hebrew word for the Pentateuch, *torah*, is often translated "law," even though *torah* is more accurately translated as "instruction" or "teaching."

Is this God who imposes hundreds of regulations on mankind not fundamentally legalistic? Let us look at the function of these laws (which is not a civil code in the modern sense of the term). Some of them are shocking:

- All rebellious sons who do not obey parental injunctions or who insult their parents must be stoned by the community (Deut 21:18–21; Exod 21:17; Lev 20:9).
- A young woman who loses her virginity before she is married must suffer the same fate and be stoned (Deut 22:13–20).
- Stoning is also prescribed for adulterous couples (Deut 22:22; Lev 20:10).
- The death penalty is inflicted in cases of sexual relations that are considered illicit (Lev 21:10).
- A father holds absolute authority over his children and can even sell them as slaves (Exod 21:7–11).

A fundamentalist or literalist reading of these texts is ethically impossible; they reflect quite obviously a society that is totally different from ours, a society that knows and accepts slavery and is built on a patriarchal ideology, a society based on the inequality of the sexes. We cannot, then, take these texts as immutable roadmaps that are relevant for all times and places. Many rabbis have also asked if stoning or other forms of killing aimed at chastisement were really applied at the time, or if they were rather a dissuasive rhetoric aimed at preventing the transgressions formulated in the Law. Their purpose, which seems to us very hard, is to protect the family unit that is located under a clearly defined hierarchy.

We must remember that in those times marriage was not a love story, but a commercial arrangement concluded between two families or clans. The prohibition of adultery is not primarily a commandment about sexual ethics, but a legal issue. In the ancient Near East, taking a wife was the equivalent of becoming her "owner." Adultery, therefore, meant a violation of the "possession" of another man. For the biblical authors, as also for the editors of the great legislative codes of Mesopotamia, adultery endangered the stability of society; that is why it is, theoretically at least, punishable by death. The fear of being the victim of adultery is also explained by the importance of descent, which was a central preoccupation. It was necessary to ensure at all costs that the offspring of a woman were those of her husband in order to guarantee the continuity of a family or clan. To mitigate this anxiety, Judaism would later adopt the idea of matrilineage, or descent along the mother's line.

In addition, let us remember that the law of retaliation (Exod 21:23–32)—that is, "an eye for an eye and a tooth for a tooth" (v 24)—though it has often been interpreted to be an ancient revenge law dictated by a bloodthirsty and vengeful god, actually helps to avoid gratuitous and disproportionate revenge and introduces the principle of reparation. In any case, an attentive reading of this same text is enough to see that the hurt inflicted can be redeemed by a cash payment (v 30). The Holiness Code (Lev 17–26) also addresses revenge from a legal perspective: "You shall not take vengeance or bear a grudge against any of your people, but you shall love your neighbor as yourself" (Lev 19:18).

If we compare the various collections of laws contained in the Pentateuch—the Decalogue in Exodus 20 and Deuteronomy 5; the Code of Alliance in Exodus 20–23; the Priestly Code in Leviticus 1–16; the Holiness Code in Leviticus 17–26; and the Deuteronomic Code in Deuteronomy 12–26—it is easy to observe that a certain number of the prescriptions are in tension with one another. Thus, the Decalogue stipulates that Yhwh will punish the faults of the fathers to the fourth generation, and supports the idea of collective responsibility. In contrast, Deuteronomy 24:16 affirms that there is no such thing as collective sanction and that each will be punished for his or her own faults. Juxtaposing these laws shows that both cannot be applied at the same time, and that it is necessary to enter into a process of interpretation when dealing with the issue of the pertinence of the two statements. The Law of the Pentateuch, therefore, is not a static set of rules: it needs to be constantly evaluated, interpreted, and even superceded.

The incident described in Leviticus 10:16–20 helps illustrate this point, so we shall mention it here. According to the interpretations of the Jewish scholars who have passed the Bible text down to us, Leviticus 10:16, the first verse of this episode, is the heart of the Torah, and in it we find the verb *darash*, "to seek," repeated twice. The implication here is that we must not merely blindly obey the Law, but we must seek proper interpretations of it. In other words, there are cases where the Law of God cannot be literally applied, and those who interpret the Law must sometimes reevaluate it in order to deal with the diversity of human circumstances.[2] In the episode itself, instead of eating the sacrificial meat that they have offered to God, as prescribed by the Law in Leviticus 6:9, Aaron and his sons simply burn it. Moses therefore accuses his brother Aaron of not respecting the Law. Aaron justifies himself by stating that two of his sons have just been killed and therefore he cannot participate in a banquet. Moses then accepts Aaron's reason, even though it is not based on a literal interpretation of the Law. Therefore, the authority of the Torah requires constant study of the Torah. The "Law" must constantly reinvent itself. This is what Jesus does in the Sermon on the Mount, as a direct extension of this concept.

When we come to deal with instructions that appear shocking or incomprehensible to us, we must remember that other laws of the Torah paint the picture of a just society, based on solidarity and opposed to all thoughts of profit and enrichment. In the context of the current crisis of capitalism, wild speculations, and exploitation of southern countries, we have to admire the general debt relief provided for in Leviticus 25 (the law of "Jubilee"; see also the seventh-year relief advocated in Deuteronomy 15), although it is probably a utopian law that was never applied. In the context of a large common market in the Persian period, this law would prevent Judea from evolving economically into a society split between an ever more prosperous minority of wealthy landowners and a large majority of smallholders who were increasingly enslaved or forced to rent themselves out to the highest bidder. At its core, the argument in Leviticus 25 rests on one central theological affirmation: the country does not belong to the people but to Yhwh, the God of Israel (v 23). For Leviticus 25, all the people are on the same footing of equality, at least theoretically, since everyone—including landlords—are *servants* of Yahweh (v 55). Other laws in the Pentateuch are also part of this concern for social justice: for example, the prohibition against taking a pledge from those who need to borrow (Deut 24:6, 10–12), or the obligation to support the weak of society materially (Deut 24:17–22).

Whereas some laws appear to us to be completely outdated, others seem to be astonishingly topical, particularly those that seek to contribute to social and economic justice. However, in regard to sexuality, it does seem as if some instructions seem to want to limit sexuality to the sole function of procreation. We will examine this next.

REPRESSED SEXUALITY?

In the first account of Creation, God orders the first couple to "be fruitful and multiply" (Gen 1:26). This order has often been interpreted as defining the sole function of human sexuality. As a result of the account of the transgression in the Garden of Eden in Genesis 3, sexuality also appears to focus on procreation, which is described here as difficult and dangerous, and legitimizing the submission of the woman to the man. Yhwh tells the woman:

> "I will greatly increase your pangs in childbearing;
>   in pain you shall bring forth children,
> yet your desire shall be for your husband,
>   and he shall rule over you." (v 16)

The passage on sexual ethics in Leviticus 18, repeated and radicalized in Leviticus 20, apparently prohibits all sexual relations that do not fit into the context of procreation: incest, adultery, sexual relations with a woman during menstruation, as well as sexual relations between two men.[3] Here we find a restrictive vision of sexuality that corresponds perhaps to the theological program of the priestly group during the Persian period.

If we had only these texts, we would have to admit that the God of the Old Testament placed no value on sexuality between human beings. But apart from them, there are sev-

103

eral other texts that indicate that sexuality is not primarily for reproduction: thus we see that Elkanah prefers his wife Hannah, who is barren, to his second wife Penninah (1 Sam 1:1–4), and Ecclesiastes counsels enjoying life with the woman that you love (Eccl 9:9). But it is particularly the Song of Solomon that defuses this negative vision of sexuality.

A HYMN TO LOVE AND EROTICISM

The Song of Solomon (or Song of Songs) is an astonishing book in the Bible. It is an erotic text, and in some passages almost pornographic (by the criteria of that period). In order to stress the importance of this canticle, those who have handed down this text have attributed it to Solomon, who in 1 Kings is presented as the author of an impressive number of poetical texts and as a lover of women. This attribution to King Solomon also facilitated the acceptance of this text into the canon of biblical books. Today, we believe that the Song of Solomon was composed in the fourth century BC. The Song makes clear reference to sensuality and to a relationship of physical love even from the first few lines: "Let him kiss me with the kisses of his mouth! / For your love is better than wine" (Song 1:2).

The text depicts two lovers who are trying to meet so that they might express their love despite several obstacles.

The Song of Solomon is decidedly not a "pious" book. Apart from one inconspicuous allusion, God is never mentioned. In order to take account of the message and of the originality of this text, we must return to the richness of the language in which it is written. But this language differs from that of all the other books in the Bible in that it describes all the different types of love, including and above all its carnal dimension. Thus, the line "His left hand is under my head, / and his right hand embraces me!"—which appears first at 2:6, and is repeated at 8:3—evokes for the ancient Near Eastern person a scene that has often been reproduced: a naked couple embracing each other before coming together (Fig. 5).

However, the message of the Song does not stop there. It wants to show that love can go beyond the inequalities between the man and the woman and give meaning to life in the face of death. In Song 7:10, the woman exclaims: "I am my beloved's, / and his desire is for me." The Hebrew word translated by *desire* is very rare in the Bible and, in fact, is found nowhere else other than Genesis 3:16 and

Fig. 5. Representation of an amorous couple, an image frequently seen throughout the ancient Near East

4:7. In the account of the fall and the expulsion of the first human couple from the Garden of Eden, God had sanctioned the woman to submit to the man: "Your desire shall be for your husband, / and he shall rule over you" (3:16). If we read the Song following this passage, we find this: In the Book of Genesis, desire appears as a punishment, while the Song celebrates desire and even reverses the roles. It is the desire of the man that leads him toward his beloved. When read mirrored with Genesis 3:16, the Song can also be understood to advocate equality of the sexes in a loving and sexual relationship. In contrast with many erotic poems, the Song describes not only the body and beauty of the woman, but also that of the man. It goes beyond the sexist and patriarchal mindset of ancient Israel, and it is also significant that it is the woman who has the first and last word in the poem.

Finally, the Song of Solomon understands love and sexuality as a gift offered to mankind that he may enjoy life despite death, which is the ineluctable destiny of humanity:

> Love is strong as death,
>   passion fierce as the grave.
> Its flashes are flashes of fire,
>   flame of Yah. (8:6)

The word *Yah* is used at the end of this verse as a discreet allusion to the proper name of the God of Israel, Yahweh. By making this reference, the author of the Song affirms that love and eroticism, which can resist death, are a divine gift that allows human beings to enjoy life, their bodies, and their amorous encounters.

CHAPTER 5

IS GOD VIOLENT AND VENGEFUL?

"In the beginning…there was violence." This is how the French philosopher Roger Dadoun expresses himself in an article, imitating the Book of Genesis.[1] In fact, it seems that right from the beginning of the Bible, God is embroiled in acts of violence. Is he not in a way the source of the first murder of humanity? A first glance at the very famous story of Cain and Abel seems to confirm this impression.

THE BIRTH OF VIOLENCE: CAIN AND ABEL

Already with chapter 4 of Genesis and the story of Cain and Abel, the biblical narrative contains violence and murder. Genesis 4 is not simply a family history; it is a myth that attempts to explain the origin of violence. The story of Cain and Abel is written based on the experience of pervasive violence and tries to explain for the reader where violence originates and how it can be dealt with. Before addressing this difficult text, let us note that Genesis 4 presupposes a situation different from the one in the previous chapter, which tells of the creation of humanity and the expulsion of the first couple from paradise. After Genesis 3, Cain and Abel should be, along with their parents, the only living beings on the earth, whereas Genesis 4 presupposes, as we will see, a widely populated land. The story of Cain and Abel, therefore, was inserted afterward into the narrative of the origins of humanity because the author of this text understood that violence is inextricably linked to the human condition. Could it be that this author lived around the seventh century BC, a period during which there was an upsurge of violence under the Assyrian occupation?

In order to thoroughly understand Genesis 4, we need to read the chapter in its entirety instead of stopping at verse 16, as is usually the case.

The Cain and Abel Account in Full

Now the man knew his wife Eve, and she conceived and bore Cain, saying, "I have produced a man with the LORD." Next she bore his brother Abel. Now Abel was a keeper of sheep, and Cain a tiller of the ground. In the course of time Cain brought to the LORD an offering of the fruit of the ground, and Abel for his part brought of the firstlings of his flock, their fat portions. And the LORD had regard for Abel and his offering, but for Cain and his offering he had no regard. So Cain was very angry, and his countenance fell. The LORD said to Cain, "Why are you angry, and why has your countenance fallen? If you do well, will you not be accepted? And if you do not do well, sin is lurking at the door; its desire is for you, but you must master it."

Cain said to his brother Abel....And when they were in the field, Cain rose up against his brother Abel, and killed him. Then the LORD said to Cain,

"Where is your brother Abel?" He said, "I do not know; am I my brother's keeper?" And the LORD said, "What have you done? Listen; your brother's blood is crying out to me from the ground! And now you are cursed from the ground, which has opened its mouth to receive your brother's blood from your hand. When you till the ground, it will no longer yield to you its strength; you will be a fugitive and a wanderer on the earth." Cain said to the LORD, "My punishment is greater than I can bear! Today you have driven me away from the soil, and I shall be hidden from your face; I shall be a fugitive and a wanderer on the earth, and anyone who meets me may kill me." Then the LORD said to him, "Not so! Whoever kills Cain will suffer a sevenfold vengeance." And the LORD put a mark on Cain, so that no one who came upon him would kill him. Then Cain went away from the presence of the LORD, and settled in the land of Nod, east of Eden.

Cain knew his wife, and she conceived and bore Enoch; and he built a city, and named it Enoch after his son Enoch. To Enoch was born Irad; and Irad was the father of Mehujael, and Mehujael the father of Methushael, and Methushael the father of Lamech. Lamech took two wives; the name of the one was Adah, and the name of the other Zillah. Adah bore Jabal; he was the ancestor of those who live in tents and have livestock. His brother's name was Jubal; he was the ancestor of all those who play the lyre and pipe. Zillah bore Tubal-cain, who made all kinds of bronze and iron tools. The sister of Tubal-cain was Naamah.

Lamech said to his wives:

"Adah and Zillah, hear my voice;
     you wives of Lamech, listen to what I say:
I have killed a man for wounding me,
     a young man for striking me.
If Cain is avenged sevenfold,
     truly Lamech seventy-sevenfold."

Adam knew his wife again, and she bore a son and named him Seth, for she said, "God has appointed for me another child instead of Abel, because Cain killed him." To Seth also a son was born, and he named him Enosh. At that time people began to invoke the name of the LORD. (Gen 4)

In many places, the text of this chapter is obscure, sometimes almost untranslatable, and this aridity perhaps reflects the difficulty the author had in understanding the phenomenon of violence and what role God plays in it. The passage has three parts that open with parallel introductions in verses 1, 17, and 25 ("Adam/Cain knew his wife").

The first part of the passage (vv 1–16) depicts fratricide and its consequences. It begins in quite a remarkable way with Eve's exclamation: "I have produced a man with the LORD." God appears here almost as a second father to Cain. How should we understand this statement?[2] Is it a fantasy of Eve's where she tries to raise herself to the same level as God? (Recall that in Genesis 3 the serpent promised her that she and her husband would become like gods). Or is it part of the male author's conflicted reaction to the fact that only women can give birth and that in doing so *they* approach the level of gods? This is the first time a double origin for Cain is suggested. Through his father Adam, he is son of the earth (in Hebrew: *'adamah*), but he is at the same time associated with the divine. But after the murder, Cain is separated from both God and the earth. Violence makes Cain doubly remote. There will no longer be any immediate relationship either with God or with nature. Moreover, the word *create* here (*qanah* in Hebrew) recalls the name Cain. Cain the murderer will also become a creator—a creator of civilization—since the word *cain*, in fact, means "javelin," "smith," or "artisan."

Through his relationship with Cain, Abel, who is apparently his twin brother, plays a much less prominent role. During the time that the text was being composed, no one would have called his son Abel, since the Hebrew word *hebel* means "mist," "little wind," or "vanity." (It is the leitmotiv of Ecclesiastes, found in its very opening: "Vanity of vanities, all is vanity.") The name Abel also contains the entire experience of the fragility of human existence. Most of all, what the text says about Abel is that he is a brother. The rivalry between brothers is a topic that we find repeated throughout world literature and it constitutes one of the major themes in the Book of Genesis (Ishmael-Isaac, Esau-Jacob, Joseph and his brothers). The account in Genesis 4 introduces the theme of rivalry with blood. It is not linked to the different professions of the two brothers (Cain the farmer against Abel the stockbreeder) as is often supposed, but comes out of the experience of inequality.

Is God the Instigator of Violence?

God recognizes Abel's sacrifice, but not Cain's. How did the brothers respond to God's reaction? The text does

not tell us; it does not even tell us what could have moti-
vated the partiality of God's choice. We often try to deni-
grate Cain by assuming, for example, that he had offered a
sacrifice of lesser quality, or that God preferred Abel because
Cain was Eve's favorite. However, the narrator does not offer
any explanation. We have to accept it and go by the evidence: there is no logical reason for God's preference. It
arises from the same kind of divine arbitrariness that we
find emphasized in Exodus 33:19: "I will be gracious to
whom I will be gracious, and will show mercy on whom I
will show mercy." However, behind this divine arbitrariness
hides our daily human experience: Life is not fair, it is
always unpredictable and it is made up of inequalities that
are not always logical and explicable. In Genesis 4, God confronts Cain with this fact that is the common experience of
everyone in life. And according to Genesis 4:5, violence
arises from Cain's incapacity to accept this inequality. The
fact that Cain is treated differently does not mean that God
rejects him, because he still speaks to him. He addresses
him as a father and—in a verse that is neither easy to understand nor easy to translate[3]—exhorts him not to give in to
sin. In Genesis 4:7, the word *sin* appears for the first time in
the Bible. According to the biblical text "original sin," therefore, is not "the story of the apple," that is, transgressing
against the divine commandment in Genesis 3.[4] The real sin
is giving free reign to violence.

However, Cain does not deal with violence. The
Hebrew text marks a break at verse 8—"Cain said to his
brother Abel…"—but what he says is not contained in the
passage. Older translations added, "Let us go out to the
field," in order to fill the gap. However, it is possible to read
this break differently. The narrator undoubtedly wanted to
get across that, after the divine exhortation, Cain tries to

speak to his brother, but does not succeed. The first murder, therefore, is also linked to the inability to communicate. It symbolizes the failure of both brothers' sacrifices. Instead of producing peace (the expression *a pleasing fragrance* is often used in priestly texts to describe the function of the sacrifice), the sacrifices, both offered spontaneously, produce an explosion of violence.

Just as he did after the transgression in the Garden of Eden, God is immediately present to question and to sanction. Cain's response—namely, the famous "Am I my brother's keeper?"—has often been interpreted as an ironic, or even cynical, attitude, as in, "Nobody asked me to look after my brother." We can also read it as if it were a cry of desperation: "How could I be my brother's keeper?" In fact, the Hebrew root *shamar* from which the word *keeper* comes is very often applied to the observance of laws. But the account of the murder is not preceded by a formal prohibition against murder. Cain utters words of confusion when confronted with violence. We ourselves have the same confusion. Like Cain, we do not always know how to deal with the outbreak of violence, whether as individuals or as a group.

Dealing with Violence

Cain is in danger of losing his bearings completely. God tells him that from now on he will be a wanderer and will be deprived of his link with the earth. Cain complains to God, who revises his judgment. "My *'awon* is too heavy to bear," the murderer exclaims. The word *'awon* can at the same time mean the sin, the crime, and the punishment. Cain understands that he is responsible for triggering the spiral of violence. "Anyone who meets me may kill me" (v 14). He who has killed fears that he will be killed in his turn. It is then that God intervenes to protect the murderer. He does this in two ways: first by stating that total vengeance will be meted out to whoever kills Cain. This first response, however, continues the inevitability of retribution and violence. Then God changes the situation again: he stops the violence by placing a sign on Cain to prevent him from being killed. The text does not tell us the nature of the sign. More important is that human life, even that of a murderer, is sacred. No human being has the right to take someone else's life. The author of Genesis 4 opposes the idea of blood revenge, which appears, for example, in Genesis 9:6: "Whoever sheds the blood of a human, by a human shall that person's blood be shed." Genesis 4:15 could almost be seen as a plea for the suppression of the death penalty. In any case, God establishes here the conditions for a nonviolent future, despite the murder that has just been committed—the primordial murder. And despite God's statement that Cain would be a wanderer, God allows him to settle in the imaginary land of Nod—a name built upon a play of words with the verb *to wander*. Cain's settlement in this land will allow the beginning of civilization to take place, as the second part of the narrative shows (vv 17–24).

Violence and Civilization

The murderer Cain had future benefits, since seven generations were descended from him. At the end of this line Jubal and Tubal-cain were born. As the similarity of their names shows, these two figures are once again understood to be twins and, like Cain and Abel, they are engaged in two different professions. Is a new beginning possible, or is history about to repeat itself?

According to the biblical account, culture and technical advancement come from the descendants of Cain. They build the first city, and their descendants invent music and metallurgy. So violence prevented neither progress nor civilization. This leads to the question of whether civilization without violence is even possible. Genesis 4 does not condemn culture; it demonstrates, instead, that culture depends on the effective management of violence. Genesis 4:16 tells us that Cain settled east of Eden. But, in Near Eastern thought, the east (where the sun rises) symbolizes life and therefore hope. Life is still possible despite violence. It remains fragile and threatened as verses 23 to 24 show. These verses tell of a descendant of Cain who perverts the sign of Cain by boasting about having killed because of a simple wound and having revived the spiral of violence.

This is why the third part of the narrative returns to Adam and Eve, who create a "replacement" for Abel. Seth will be the father of Enosh, whose name simply means "humanity." Does this story end in the hope of a new humanity? The narrator tells us that it is under Enosh that the name of Yhwh begins to be invoked. He opposes the "silent" sacrifice of Cain and Abel at the beginning of the story. The word *invoke* (*qara'*) is an act of communication with God that involves words. Thus, to deal with violence, human beings are called to worship through words, which in the Hebrew Bible are lived out through the reading of the Law and through seeking an appropriate ethic to live by.

Violence and the Human Condition

According to Genesis 4, violence is part of the human condition. It originates from the fact that human beings are unable to tolerate distinctions or inequalities between each other. Nevertheless, God is no stranger to this violence, since he requires human beings to confront the inequality that causes violence. But God also wants human beings to learn to deal with violence instead of escalating it. Violence, like freedom and responsibility, make up part of the human condition. And as God is no stranger to any area of human life, he is also involved in the violence, always giving human beings a means of "escape." Dealing with violence does not mean denying or withdrawing from the conflicts that define our lives and times. Confronting violence, means getting involved.

GOD OF VENGEANCE?

Calls to vengeance in the Bible can strike us as an extremely shocking form of verbal violence. The Psalter contains a number of psalms of vengeance whose sentiments can scandalize modern readers. In these texts, an appeal is made to God to punish the enemies of the Psalmist, and in some psalms we find divine titles like "avenger" (Ps 99:8) or "God of vengeance" (Ps 94:1), accompanied by particularly cruel images. These appeals for vengeance can be found, on the one hand, in psalms in which the individual addresses God, and, on the other, in psalms that are communal prayers.

The Appeal for Vengeance
in the Communal Psalms

Psalm 137 commemorates the despair of the exiles in Babylon. It must have been written during the Persian period at the earliest, because there is a time difference between the situation in Babylon and the Psalmist. The Psalmist is not in Babylon, but remembers the experience of exile. Babylon, in this psalm, could be generally interpreted to symbolize the Jewish people's various experiences of exile and oppression. Indeed, over the last centuries BC, Babylon became a symbol for hostile empires; it is used, for instance, to refer to the Roman Empire, as in the Revelation of St.

John. This could be confirmed by the mention of Edom in verse 7, which in the rabbinical tradition symbolizes the people hostile to Babylon. But in the context of the Persian era, the mention of Edom also makes sense, because the Edomites profited from the Babylonians' destruction of Jerusalem and Judah by occupying a part of Judea.

In any case, in this psalm, Babylon represents the capital of the world, and the psalm itself reflects the experience of the Jews in exile there, which will be a common experience for Judaism throughout its history.

The first part of the psalm describes the situation of the musicians deported to Babylon (a rather common practice as shown in Assyrian bas-reliefs):

> By the rivers[5] of Babylon—
>   there we sat down and there we wept
>   when we remembered Zion. (Ps 137:1)

The first few verses of this psalm are very beautiful, which explains why they have also been used in Christian hymnody. But if we take a look at the end of the psalm, we can only be shocked by the final wishes that the author expresses with regard to Babylon:

> O daughter Babylon, you devastator!
>   Happy shall they be who pay you back
>   what you have done to us!
> Happy shall they be who take your little ones
>   and dash them against the rock! (vv 8–9)

It is hardly surprising that these last verses are often removed from liturgical readings of Psalm 137. In the Jewish tradition, the orthodox Ashkenazi read the entire psalm daily, whereas conservative and liberal Jews omit the last three verses. This corresponds to what the Catholic Church has chosen for the Liturgy of the Hours.

How can we justify such appeals to vengeance? These verses have given rise to all sorts of reactions and explanations, including anti-Semitic ones, as in a commentary from the beginning of the twentieth century that sees in these texts a typical expression of an archaic Judaism "taken up with hatred and vengeance." Some Fathers of the Church (notably Origen) have put forward an allegorical reading and interpret the little ones of Babylon as a symbol of sinful thoughts that must be destroyed with the greatest firmness. Some others have justified this wish as the punishment merited by the Babylonians. But can we really think this way? We must remember that the practice of crushing the small children of a vanquished town was (unfortunately) one of the customs of war in antiquity.

Consider Nahum 3:10, which tells of the Babylonian victory over Nineveh:

> Yet she became an exile,
>   she went into captivity;
> even her infants were dashed in pieces
>   at the head of every street;
> lots were cast for her nobles,
>   all her dignitaries were bound in fetters.

Isaiah 13:16 also announces the destruction of Babylon with the following words:

> Their infants will be dashed to pieces
>   before their eyes;
> their houses will be plundered,
>   and their wives ravished.

This act of barbarism was aimed at eliminating (probably in symbolic terms) the descendants of a town in order to prevent it from becoming powerful again one day. The Psalmist expresses his thirst for vengeance with an image that reflects the practices that were current at that time.

The exclamation in Psalm 137:8–9 should be understood as nothing but an expression of deep turmoil. God and his justice appear to be far away, while a foreign power is oppressing the people. What can the oppressed do when they do not even have the means to mount any kind of revolt? All they can do is protest verbally. It is easy to see that they cannot act in a measured, ethical, and politically correct way. Verse 9 expresses the hope that the power of oppression might disappear, deprived of new generations. Therefore, this is how we should understand such a shocking appeal to kill children: it reflects a situation of distress in which all one can do is cry out about one's suffering. But the perversion—indeed, the blasphemy—happens when a cry of despair (almost as a provocation to God) is transformed into a political agenda aimed at the destruction of enemies. If taken out of context, these appeals to vengeance are unacceptable, and it is undoubtedly right not to read them in celebrations that have nothing to do with the situation of the Psalmist.

Can We Speak of God the Judge?

Psalm 136 opens with an appeal to the Creator God:

O give thanks to the LORD, for he is good,
    for his steadfast love endures forever.
O give thanks to the God of gods,
    for his steadfast love endures forever.

But a little further on in the same psalm, there is an exhortation to praise God because he massacres others:

> O give thanks to the LORD, for he is good,
>   for his steadfast love endures forever…
> who struck down great kings,
>   for his steadfast love endures forever;
> and killed famous kings,
>   for his steadfast love endures forever.
>   (vv 1, 17–18)

Again, we may be disturbed by God killing kings and powerful people. But what happens if we "translate" this sentiment into a more historically recent setting, such as the collapse of Nazi Germany during World War II?

> O give thanks to the Lord, for he is good, for his steadfast love endures forever…who definitively wiped out the Wehrmacht 6th Army at Stalingrad, for his steadfast love endures forever; and who doomed Nazi Germany to destruction, for his steadfast love endures forever.[6]

Few people would condemn the above prayer. In the same way, the violent lines in Psalm 136 express an idea that is central to biblical tradition: God intervenes on behalf of the oppressed and is violently opposed to the oppressor. This is what the song of Hannah in the Old Testament expresses, in 1 Samuel 2:1–10, and also the Magnificat in the New Testament, in Luke 1:47–55. Some of the biblical passages that speak of God's violent intervention could be appropriate for those who find themselves in a situation in which they are oppressed or who are emerging from oppression.[7] Of course, this is not to say that it is appropriate to use these psalms to construct a theology that condones, as a matter of doctrine, the intentional destruction of innocent people for the profit or benefit of the aggressor.

We have now dealt with the psalms that express the situation of a group of people. But some of the psalms are also individual appeals for vengeance.

Psalms with Personal Appeals for Vengeance

Psalm 58 reflects the situation of an individual surround by "wicked" people who are violating his rights and practicing injustice (see vv 2–3). He prays:

> O God, break the teeth in their mouths....
> The righteous will rejoice when they see vengeance
>   done;
>   they will bathe their feet in the blood of the
>   wicked.
> People will say, "Surely there is a reward for the
>   righteous;
>   surely there is a God who judges on earth."
>   (vv 6, 10–11)

A passage like this is difficult, and the fact that similar prayers were made by tribes who were Israel's neighbors changes nothing. It is undoubtedly an appeal for violent vengeance. Before we analyze the function of these verses, we must first emphasize the fact that the structure of Psalm 58 reveals a displacement as to the question of justice. The beginning of the psalm criticizes the actions of the powerful: "Your hands deal out violence on earth" (v 2), whereas the Psalmist proclaims at the end: "Surely there is a God who judges on earth." This means that the principle statement of the psalm is an affirmation of divine justice, despite all evidence.

What is shocking in this psalm is the aggressiveness the Psalmist uses when describing the fate that awaits the wicked. We cannot solve this theological problem by countering this warlike psalm with the message of love brought by the New Testament, because the Apocalypse of John also refers to joy when faced with God's judgment against Babylon, the great prostitute (Rev 18:20), and describes the anger of God as an unimaginable bloodbath (14:20). Nor can we solve the problem by deciding that verse 11 was added during the Maccabean period (from the second century BC), during which a spirit of revenge was prevalent, thereby concluding that this vengefulness was merely a characteristic of the time.

Here, as in other psalms, the author identifies his enemies as the enemies of God. This is dangerous, because identifying human interests with those of God could be a source of fanaticism and terrible violence. However, we must also note that the Psalmist relies on God to carry out vengeance, which, in Psalm 58, is the same as establishing justice, despite the cruelest of images. The act of transferring the desire for revenge to God allows the Psalmist to undergo a sort of catharsis. By placing his desire for vengeance onto God, the Psalmist is in effect relieved of it, thus *preventing* violence. In the story of Cain and Abel, God stops vengeance in order to prevent the murderer Cain from being killed in his turn. The Apostle Paul well understood this mechanism: "Beloved, never avenge yourselves, but leave room for the wrath of God; for it is written, 'Vengeance is mine, I will repay, says the Lord'" (Rom 12:19, which reiterates Deut 32:35). So handing over the desire for violence and vengeance to God can have a therapeutic function.

God of Vengeance or God of Love?

These comments are not intended to trivialize biblical texts that appeal for divine vengeance. We must uphold these texts, but also remain attentive to the fact that they are not applicable in every situation. The authors of the Old Testament were already aware of the danger of this vengeful ideology, which is why Leviticus 19:18 warns against vengeful feelings with regard to one's neighbor: "You shall not take vengeance or bear a grudge against any of your people, but you shall love your neighbor as yourself." In a general way, the Bible itself shows that we cannot limit God to a condition where he is automatically violently opposed to those who are opposed to him.

The account of the flood (Gen 6–9) shows an interesting change in regards to the divine behavior. God first responds to humanity's violence with the violence of the flood. But in the end, God himself prohibits the possibility of such vengeance: "I will never again curse the ground because of humankind, for the inclination of the human heart is evil from youth; nor will I ever again destroy every living creature as I have done" (Gen 8:21).

From the beginning, the Bible insists on the primacy of divine love. This balances all the texts that portray God as judge. The divine oracle in Hosea 11:9 clearly states: "I will not execute my fierce anger....for I am God and no mortal."

CHAPTER 6

IS GOD COMPREHENSIBLE?

"What did I do to God to deserve that?"

Everyone has at one time heard or used this rhetorical question. However, the origins of this exclamation, often used by people who would call themselves nonbelievers, comes from the conviction that God is responsible for all the misfortunes that befall us. The same question is often uttered at a communal level when a disaster hits a country or a people: "If there is a God and if God is love, why are there wars, famines, and natural disasters?" Behind these questions, there is a hidden quest for the logic of divine behavior. If God has made creation "very good," as it says in the first chapter of the Bible, why do misfortune and suffering exist?

One way of explaining the presence of evil is as a punishment for bad behavior. God is then thought of as the supreme disciplinarian and all misfortune is deserved misfortune. We will see that these ideas are present in the Old Testament, and also in the New Testament. Their aim, in fact, is to make God and evil comprehensible. However, the authors of the Hebrew Bible were aware of the dangers of this kind of thinking.

IS GOD ON THE SIDE
OF THE JUST?

The psalms begin with a description of the "ideal man":

Happy are those
   who do not follow the advice of the wicked,
or take the path that sinners tread....
They are like trees
   planted by streams of water....
In all that they do, they prosper.

The wicked are not so,
   but are like chaff that the wind drives away...
for the LORD watches over the way of the righteous,
   but the way of the wicked will perish.
     (Ps 1:1, 3, 4, 6)

This beatitude presents two types of persons: those who are successful because they conform themselves to the will of God (Ps 1:2), and the others, sinners and the wicked. This opposition between the "just" and the "wicked" we find in many of the psalms that insist on the fact that God is with the just but punishes the wicked:

Do not let the slanderer be established in the land;
   let evil speedily hunt down the violent!....
Surely the righteous shall give thanks to your name;
   the upright shall live in your presence."
     (Ps 140:11–13)

This separation of human beings into two categories allows us to rationalize all misfortunes since they are nothing but a divine punishment for sinners. This idea has its roots in the sapiential, or wisdom, tradition of Israel,[1] as can be found principally in the Book of Proverbs. In Proverbs 13:21, we read: "Misfortune pursues sinners, / but prosperity rewards the righteous." This saying sums up the whole theory of retribution, according to which God guarantees the link between the behavior of an individual and his fate. In short, good people prosper while wicked people suffer.

The origin of this idea lies in a belief shared by all the sages from the ancient Near East. According to this belief, the universe is not a game of chance; it is the work of God the Creator, and a cosmic order established by God reigns over it. Consequently, it is up to the wise person to discover the principles of this world order and comply with them by contributing to the task of preserving that order. This sort of attitude ensures a harmonious and prosperous life. A foolish and vengeful attitude causes an imbalance in the created order of things and leads to harmful consequences. In Egypt, this cosmic order, to which wise people try to conform, is called *ma'at*.

Ma'at appears in Egyptian iconography as a young woman with a headdress, representing the hieroglyph of her name, namely, an upright feather (Fig. 6). In biblical Hebrew, the equivalent terms for the cosmic order are *shalom* (which is often translated as "peace," but whose meaning is more global) and *tsedaqah*, often translated as "justice." Someone who lives in harmony with order is *tsadik*, or "just." The connotation of the adjective *just* in this case is not, strictly speaking, legalistic, but rather relational. The *tsadik* is someone who lives in harmony with the order of the world and of society, and who with God guarantees that order.

The idea of a God who is on the side of the just is not an abstract doctrine. It arises from the observation of daily facts:

whoever sows will reap, whoever promotes good relationships with his neighbor will
be valued, and so on. These
observations are summed up
in Proverbs 24:12: "Does not
he who keeps watch over
your soul [that is, God]
know it? / And will he not
repay all according to their
deeds?" The sapiential, or
wisdom, vision of the world
is resolutely optimistic,
because it starts with the
principle that through observation and teaching the
wise person can understand
the rules of the universe.

Fig. 6. Representation of the
Egyptian *ma'at*

However, true wisdom remains aware that the task will
always prove too much for human beings. The sages knew
that their wisdom had limits. Proverbs 20:24 states this
clearly: "All our steps are ordered by the LORD; / how then
can we understand our own ways?"

This "empirical" wisdom, based on observation of the
world, was threatened by a danger that assails all discussion
about God: dogmatism. This is particularly the case with
Proverbs 10–15, which undoubtedly once constituted a separate collection, and which clearly contains a kind of dogmatism. Within these chapters are many sentences that do
not describe concrete behaviors required to achieve certain
consequences, but rather contrast two types of people and
the fate that awaits them. For example: "When the storm is
over, the wicked is no more, / but the upright stands firm

forever (Prov 10:25). It is a sort of black and white picture that divides humanity into two categories: the wise and the foolish, the just and the wicked; a sort of dualism develops. On the side of God we find order and the just; on the other there is nothing but chaos and the wicked. And God, quite obviously, gives well-being to the just, while misfortune and suffering are reserved for the wicked.

The dogma of retribution will itself become so powerful that some will not hesitate to rewrite history. According to 2 Kings, Manasseh was the most dreadful of all the monarchs who had governed Judah. However, his reign was the longest of all the Judean kings, fifty-five years (2 Kgs 21:1). For the author of 1 and 2 Chronicles, this is intolerable. Manasseh should have been punished by Yhwh for his bad actions. So, in order to explain the fifty-five years of Manasseh's reign, the Chronicler tells us how, at its beginning, Manasseh was converted to Yhwh; it is, therefore, thanks to this conversion that God prolonged his reign (2 Chr 33:11–13). For the Chronicler, this story was necessary in order to understand the length of this king's reign; it is important for him that Manasseh must be part of the just. And thus the world was "in order."

The idea of retribution is reassuring, because it seems to make God and the world comprehensible. This concept is not just limited to Old Testament times. In the New Testament, it appears to be well established, because the disciples question Jesus about a blind man, asking: "Rabbi, who sinned, this man or his parents, that he was born blind?"[2] Even in our times, some well-meaning people show the same attitude when they say that AIDS is God's punishment inflicted on those who lead a debauched life. If the protagonists of this idea had read the Hebrew Bible more attentively, they would have noticed that the dogma of retribution gave rise to radical doubts over this principle.

THE PROBLEM OF THE CONCEPT OF RETRIBUTION

To say that "misfortune pursues sinners, / but prosperity rewards the righteous" (Prov 13:21) is one thing, but what about times when personal experience contradicts this axiom—that is, when good people suffer? Many psalms explore this connection between a person's behavior and their fate. For example:

> For I was envious of the arrogant;
>   I saw the prosperity of the wicked.
>
> For they have no pain;
>   their bodies are sound and sleek.
> They are not in trouble as others are;
>   they are not plagued like other people. (Ps 73:3–5)

The Book of Job

In the Book of Job, the problem of retribution and of a retributive God is expressed with such power that it is impossible to discuss the theological implications of biblical retribution without taking Job into account. It is not surprising that Job is one of the books that has never stopped speaking to humankind, to believers as well as nonbelievers, to philosophers and anthropologists,[3] even to authors of novels and science fiction.[4] In fact, the question of the degree to which we can actually understand God could be considered one of the great theological problems of humanity. This problem becomes particularly acute at times of economic, social, and political crisis. It is no accident that the economic and ideological crises of today's industrial societies raise questions concerning values and meaning. For the author of Job, the crisis over the traditional understanding of God is linked to the globalization of the world and the upheaval in traditional structures that were taking place during the Persian period.

As we have said, the experience of an incomprehensible God was not particular to the Jewish faith. This is why Job is not portrayed as an Israelite. The author locates the story partly in Arabia, at the edge of the habitable lands, on the fringes of the desert, where the ordered world is threatened by chaos.[5] It is within this paradigmatic framework that the encounter between Job and God takes place. This comes about in a very different way within the narrative (1:1—2:13; 42:7–17), which in a way maintains the idea of retribution. In the main section of the book (3:1—42:6), which is in verse form, Job goes so far as to accuse God of acting against him for no reason (7:20). It is often thought that the poetic and the narrative elements of the book are the work of two different authors, and this is highly possible. It is also possible that there was only one author, and this person bracketed the rather unorthodox poetical protests against God in chapters 3 to 42 with a more traditional narrative in order to make his central message—calling into question the intelligibility of God—more palatable to his audience. Note again that in the central poem, God is very rarely called Yhwh, but instead El, Eloah, and Shaddai. God is not depicted as the God of Israel, but is rather the international, universal God.

The main part of the Book of Job consists of discourses or speeches: of Job himself, of his friends, and of God. His friends, who represent traditional theology, are convinced that Job's suffering has come about as a punishment for some hidden sin; therefore, they exhort Job to recognize his fault, cast himself on God's mercy, and repent. Here we need to emphasize an important point that commentators often neglect: that it is Job and not his friends who first brings up the idea of divine retribution. Addressing them, he exclaims: "Teach me, and I will be silent; / make me understand how I have gone wrong" (6:24). He is convinced that he is innocent, that he is "just," and he believes that he does not deserve his fate. Like his friends, Job is trying to find out what has caused the terrible situation in which he finds himself. But in contrast to his friends, Job attempts to explain his sufferings as a result of God's aggressiveness and wickedness. "You have turned cruel to me; / with the might of your hand you persecute me" (30:21). And it is in rebelling against God that Job finds that there is no divinely ordained relationship between cause and effect. "The wicked are spared in the day of calamity, / and are rescued in the day of wrath" (21:30). Nevertheless, Job is not content with this explanation; he never stops claiming that he is innocent and defies God to answer him (31:35).

The Book of Job ends with a theophany from God—a final response to Job. At some point during the development of the book, a separate editor inserted between Job's last speech and God's final response the comments of another man, Elihu, who tries to explain the sufferings of the just man as means by which God teaches (cf. 36:15). This insertion shows that a later editor wanted to provide an interpretative framework for the response God is about to give, probably because it seemed a little obscure to him.

In fact, God's reply has much intrigued commentators. First, it seems to skirt the question of suffering. God does not respond directly to Job's concerns, but instead asks Job some questions, and also engages in the kind of self-praise that can be found in the psalms that sing of the glory of God the Creator. His response to Job can be broken into two speeches (38:1—40:2 and 40:6—41:26). Let's take a closer look at the two.

In the first speech, God addresses Job with ironic questions that make Job appear, in his ignorance, incapable of understanding God and his creation. In the same speech, God presents himself as the ruler of the animals. In a remarkable book, Swiss theologian Othmar Keel has interpreted the text of Job 39 as coming out of Near Eastern iconography.[6] The author of the Book of Job appears to be employing the very common theme of the "Lord of the animals," a motif that presents a central hero taming two or more threatening beasts (Fig. 7). Most of the animals mentioned in God's speech are present in these ancient Near Eastern representations: ibex, deer, buffalo, ostriches, and others. This theme of asserting control over dangerous animals is an artistic expression of the universal sovereignty of a king or a god over all things under him. Jeremiah 27:6 uses this very theme to express the absolute power that

Fig. 7. The "Lord of the animals."
Representation from the Persian period

Yhwh confers on the Babylonian king. Thus, by taking up this theme in Job 39, the author is stressing primarily the sovereignty of God and the fact that he is not answerable to anyone. At the same time, the beasts subdued by the "Lord of the animals" could symbolize the forces of chaos, which threaten the world that has been ordered by the Creator God.

The battle against chaos is consequently the subject of God's *second* speech (40:6—41:26), which mentions the famous creatures Behemoth and Leviathan. There has been considerable scholarly discussion of the identity of these creatures, which have sometimes been translated as "hippopotamus" and "crocodile." But translating them this way obscures their mythological connotations. We could see in these two monsters the Egyptian god of the underworld, Seth, who according to myth is defeated by Horus. However, it seems more probable that their origin derives from Canaanite mythology. In this case, Leviathan may be the "Lotan" of the Ugaritic texts, which is one of the manifestations of aquatic chaos that the Creator God must battle against (Fig. 8). In any case, God's second speech confronts Job with a God who must constantly battle against the forces of chaos. It is true that God has created the world (this is the primary theme of the first speech), and that he is all-powerful. But the victory over chaos is never definitive: God must always come against it. The idea held by Job and his friends—that evil could come directly from God—is denounced here. The divine speeches make it clear that the forces of evil have their own independent existence, and that this evil is independent of God.

Is Job convinced? His response to God's second speech (42:1–6) raises many philosophical and exegetical questions. The *Jerusalem Bible* translates the end of his reply as "I retract what I have said, / and repent in dust and ashes." A

Fig. 8. Assyrian representation of God the
Creator confronting sea monsters

more literal translation would read, "I have lost all interest
and I regret [or: have changed my mind about] the dust and
ashes."⁷ This would mean perhaps that Job had abandoned
the quest for a comprehensible God and that he regrets the
symbol of his mourning, or that he accepts a world whose
ways are not open to human understanding. In so doing, he
paves the way for the biblical Book of Ecclesiastes.

The Book of Ecclesiastes

Ecclesiastes accepts the very thing that Job revolts
against: the absence of a divine guarantee that someone's
behavior and their destiny will be linked: "There are righteous people who are treated according to the conduct of the
wicked, and there are wicked people who are treated according to the conduct of the righteous" (Eccl 8:14). Ecclesiastes
even seems critical of Job: "It is known what human beings
are, and that they are not able to dispute with those who are
stronger. The more words, the more vanity" (6:10–11).

Ecclesiastes accepts the idea that God is incomprehensible, but the author goes further and confuses God with destiny. The word *destiny* (in Hebrew, *miqrah*), which appears in neither Proverbs nor Job, appears seven times in Ecclesiastes. Like the deists of the Enlightenment, Ecclesiastes believes that God is the author of the world, but that this world is incomprehensible nevertheless.

However, faced with this remote God, Ecclesiastes speaks of the "fear of God." In contrast to its meaning in conventional wisdom, this term has lost any overtones of confidence or optimism. In Ecclesiastes, fear expresses a sense of distance and submission to a remote power. This is one way to react when faced with a God who is unknown and unknowable.

Ecclesiastes, who lived in the third century BC, at the point when Hellenistic culture was everywhere in Palestine, is perhaps the first philosopher of Judaism. He conducts a rigorous enquiry into the meaning of life that is far more coherent than what the majority of his exegetes assume. To him, life seems absurd to the point where the search for meaning is left unanswered. In fact, the word *hebel* can be translated as "absurd"; it appears at the opening of the book and is currently translated as "vanity."[8] For Ecclesiastes, this does not give rise to gloomy pessimism, because he often appeals to joy: "I know that there is nothing better for them than to be happy and enjoy themselves as long as they live" (3:12), while also emphasizing man's ignorance about the things of God: "Just as you do not know how the breath comes...so you do not know the work of God, who makes everything" (11:5). This concept resists the easy image of God; Ecclesiastes' insistence on God's inscrutability, and therefore on God's inability to be "used," is opposed to the sort of faith that becomes an ideology, a faith that seeks to appropriate God.

The acceptance of Ecclesiastes into the canon of sacred

scripture was not an obvious choice for Judaism, and it is easy to see why. Ecclesiastes' God seems so remote from the God of the patriarchs and the God of the exodus who reveals himself to his people and communicates the rules of life to them through the Torah. However, the inclusion of Ecclesiastes in the canon, just like the inclusion of Job, shows that Judaism was aware of the reality of the "hidden God." Behind this reality hides a theological problem for all time concerning the relationship between God and evil.

GOD AND EVIL

We have seen how traditional Israelite thought tended to explain misfortune and suffering as God's punishment for the faults of an individual or a people. The Book of Job and the Book of Ecclesiastes refute this explanation, which was based on the idea of retribution. This raises the issue of the "status" of evil in relation to God, the creator of the universe. In God's speeches in the Book of Job, the powers of chaos that represent evil are described as independent in origin from God, who has to combat them.

There is a similar idea in the priestly account of Creation in Genesis 1. The author insists that the world created by God was to be good. As it now exists, however, the world does not conform to God's original plan. These deviations from God's original creation are made clear in the account of the flood and in the conclusion of the alliance with Noah (Gen 9:1–7).[9] The biblical account of the flood, in contrast to many other parallel texts that are found in the ancient Near East, identified human wickedness as the motivating factor for God's initiative and gives him an ethical dimension. However, the narrative does not speculate on the origins of evil. For the priestly author of the first Creation narrative, the answer to this question is clear: God did not create evil! Before God creates through his word, there was the *tohu–bohu*, the *tehom* (that is, the primordial waters)—two expressions that symbolize chaos—and darkness (Gen 1:2). God integrates these into creation by transforming them (the waters are pushed back; the darkness is made light), but the darkness and the chaos are not good (on the first day of Creation it is only the light that is called good, Gen 1:4). Genesis 1, then, shows a tendency to exclude evil from God's work.

The autonomy of evil in relation to God is affirmed in several strands of Judaism from the Persian period, most notably in the figure of Satan. The substantive *Satan* could be translated "attacker" or "adversary." In the prologue to the Book of Job, Job's sufferings are explained as a result of a wager between God and Satan, who appears as a celestial agent provocateur. This view reflects a departure from the central poem in Job 3–40, in which neither Job nor God makes reference to any incarnation of evil.

The same tendency to make evil autonomous is apparent in the First Book of Chronicles, in the narrative where David takes a census that ends up angering God and provoking divine punishment. The original text in 2 Samuel 24 begins like this: "Again *the anger of the* LORD was kindled against Israel, and he incited David against them." On the other hand, 1 Chronicles 21:1 introduces the same story with: "*Satan* stood up against Israel, and incited David to count the people of Israel." Satan then becomes an agent of God's anger. We can hardly say that Satan, in these texts, is operating in a way that is totally independent of God. In the prologue of Job, he is clearly functioning under Yhwh's orders, a kind of secret agent. In the passage in Chronicles, it is possible that Satan is nothing more than the personification of God's incomprehensible side. Seeing Satan as the primary protagonist of evil has led to a dualist tendency where evil appears almost as powerful as God, the creator of good. This dualist tendency in the Christian religion became prominent in the Middle Ages, and has given rise to all sorts of fantasies about the devil, which we find today in some science fiction films but also in political speeches that speak of pitting the forces of good against the forces of evil.

In order to counter such dualistic aberrations, Deutero-Isaiah then defends the notion that God created evil:

> I am the LORD, and there is no other;
>> besides me there is no god.
>> I arm you, though you do not know me,
> so that they may know, from the rising of the sun
>> and from the west, that there is no one besides me;
>> I am the LORD, and there is no other.
> I form light and create darkness,
>> I make weal and create evil [ra'];
>> I the LORD do all these things. (45:5–7)

This is the only text in the Bible (with the possible exception of Eccl 7:14) that explicitly states that God not only created "weal" (*shalom* or "harmonious order)," but also its opposite, evil or chaos. It is not by chance that this statement comes in the second part of the Book of Isaiah, since, as we have highlighted several times, it is Deutero-Isaiah who affirms most clearly monotheism and the uniqueness of God. The passage we have just quoted is part of an oracle concerning the Persian king Cyrus whom Deutero-Isaiah presents as God's Messiah (45:1–7), maintaining that the Persian power is serving the God of Israel. The Persian religion, Mazdeism, was marked by a strong dualism. It is against this dualism, which had undoubtedly tempted his compatriots, that Deutero-Isaiah takes a position. Because there is only one God, and apart from him there is nothing, nothing can escape this God.

It is true that this affirmation does not resolve the questions Job and some of the psalmists raise, nor our questions about the meaning of suffering; on the contrary, the diversity of biblical discourses on the relationship between God and evil confronts us with an insoluble theological problem. If we do not wish to "satanize" evil, we are left with the incomprehensible side of the biblical God, as John Chrysostom expresses in his treatise "On the Incomprehensibility of Divine Nature."[10] But this does not permit us to intellectually abuse the idea of an incomprehensible God in order to justify a fatalistic position, either ethically or theologically. Job and Ecclesiastes want to teach us to resist the temptation to dwell on the idea of retribution. In doing so, they want to jolt us out of our anthropocentric view of God and of Creation, inviting us at the same time to allow ourselves to be surprised by the God of the Bible.

A GOD OF SURPRISES

The Hebrew Bible shows us both a God who makes a covenant with his people and defines the rules of play—as well as a God who acts in a surprising manner and who is ready to call into question the legalism of these rules when applied by humankind.

Let us examine the encounter between Elijah and God. This encounter takes place in a rather unorthodox way when compared with the usual settings of biblical theophanies in which God reveals himself to humankind. In 1 Kings 18, Elijah wins a dazzling victory over the prophets of Baal thanks to a spectacular intervention by Yhwh in the form of celestial fire. But in 1 Kings 19, Elijah flees Queen Jezebel and comes to the mountain of God, like a second Moses (v 8). Tired of being oppressed, he begins to question himself over the issue of exclusive worship of Yhwh. Then God says to him, "Go out and stand on the mountain before the LORD, for the LORD is about to pass by" (v 11). Elijah and the reader then wait for God to manifest his power to reassure the prophet in his time of crisis. In fact, there then follows a parade of the traditional elements of theophany: a hurricane, an earthquake, and a fire. But Yhwh is not to be found in any of these cosmic elements (unlike the manifestation on Sinai in Exod 19). He appears in what could be literally translated as "a voice of silence," a breath that is almost inaudible and imperceptible. This is at least a surprising divine manifestation, which does not correspond to any of the traditional theophanies. A contrast is therefore established between the force of the cosmic elements and the feebleness of a voice that is almost silence. It is nonetheless the means chosen by God to enter into contact with Elijah. Historical analysis allows us to read this episode as a polemic against the worship of Baal, the god of storm, whose worship was widespread throughout the Levant. It is also perhaps a polemic against the worship of Yhwh as though *he* were a *baal*. We could also read this text as a warning against a theology of strong emotions. Further, 1 Kings 19 invites the reader to accept that God can come to mankind in a way that is neither triumphant, nor easy to understand.

The experience of a surprising God is also the theme of the Book of Jonah. This masterpiece was without doubt written in the fourth or third century BC. With fine irony, the author denounces a self-centered concept of God. At the same time, he opposes the theology inherited from the Deuteronomistic school of thought that would like to confine God to the logic of sanction and retribution. The narrator chooses as his hero a nationalist prophet from the eighth century BC who is mentioned in 2 Kings 14:25. Through Jonah, the reader is lead to rethink the traditional notions about God. At the beginning of the narrative, Jonah imagines that he can flee from the presence of Yhwh (Jonah 1:3) as though he were linked to a specific place. Jonah does not take into account the irony of his behavior when he confesses before the pagan sailors that Yhwh is God of the heavens, and creator of the sea and of the continents (Jonah 1:9). Unlike Jonah, it is the pagans who adopt the correct attitude toward God by fearing him and worshipping him in the middle of the ocean.

In most of the prophetic books of the Hebrew Bible, there are collections of oracles against the nations. These are presented in such a way as to give the impression that the restoration of Israel requires first the judgment of the nations. But in the Book of Jonah, Nineveh, which symbolizes all the threats that the Hebrew people had to face, is not destroyed by God, despite the oracle of judgment that God obliges the prophet to proclaim. The pagan sailors understand before Jonah does when they exclaim, "You, O LORD, have done as it pleased you" (1:14). Jonah, on the other hand, accuses God of discrediting him by not bringing about the destruction he had announced (4:1–3). God then undertakes to educate the prophet by showing him that his freedom and his mercy break the bonds of causality in which humanity is always tempted to enclose him.[11] This small book, which is somewhat marginal to the collection of the prophetic books, contains a fundamental key to understanding the God of the Hebrew Bible: ultimately, the will of God is to save the whole of humankind.

THE GOD OF THE OLD AND THE NEW TESTAMENTS

In the course of our brief survey on God in the Old Testament, we have said little about the God who frees his people, who enters into a special relationship with Israel, and who, according to the prophets, is constantly exhorting humanity to live in peace and social justice. In the same prophetic books, he announces an age of universal peace in which Egypt, Assyria, and Israel will be reconciled (Isa 19). These are the aspects that are rightly emphasized in the traditional "theologies of the Old Testament." However, our aim was not to add to these theological syntheses, but rather to examine those aspects of God that readers of the Hebrew Bible find disturbing or even worthy of rejection. By stressing those texts that present God as apparently bullying, cruel, warlike, and incomprehensible, we have undoubtedly taken a risk, since one could conclude that here is further proof that the God of the Old Testament has nothing to do with the God of the New Testament. However, we hope that an examination of these difficult passages shows that they were written in very particular historical situations. Often, these texts aimed at warning their readers against ideas about God that are too human and that stress the limits of theological thinking.

The relationship between the two Testaments of the Christian Bible is still a valid subject for discussion. An existential approach to the Bible, like that of German theologian Rudolf Bultmann (1884–1976) and his disciples, highlights the discontinuity between the two Testaments. For Bultmann, the history of the Jewish people and of the Law is a failure and contrasts with the New Testament proclamation of justification by faith, without works. The interpretation of Swiss scripture scholar Wilhelm Vischer (1895–1988) is different and it strongly emphasizes continuity.[1] According to Vischer, the New Testament is the logical outcome of the Old because all the promises contained in the latter point to the coming of Jesus the Messiah.

Although the interpretations of Bultmann and Vischer are diametrically opposite, both have the same starting point: they read the Old Testament in relation to the New, and therefore do not consider it independently. But suppose we look at it from a different perspective and read the New Testament in the light of what Christian terminology calls the Old Testament. This seems more plausible, since the Bible of the first generation of Christians was exclusively the Old Testament (most often in Greek translation).[2] And no New Testament writing could replace the Bible of the Jewish people. At the risk of exaggerating, I would even say that many of the New Testament texts are designed according to the Jewish tradition of *midrashim* (the *midrash* being a practical and interpretative rewriting of the texts of the Hebrew Bible). Thus, the Gospel of Matthew can be read as a midrash of the Pentateuch: it contains five parts and presents Jesus as a new Moses.[3] According to the evangelist Luke, the Law and the prophets remain the mandatory reference point for all Christians. So, in the Parable of the Rich Man and Lazarus, Abraham tells the rich man (who is suffering in hell and who wants to warn his brothers away from the same fate): "If they do not listen to Moses and the prophets, neither will they be convinced even if someone rises from the dead" (Luke 16:31).

Therefore, without question, the God of the evangelists or of Paul is the same as the God of the authors of the Hebrew Bible. Besides, the several questions that we have raised concerning the God of the Old Testament could also have been asked of the God of the New Testament. Is God "male"? The New Testament presents God as "father" more frequently than the Old Testament does. Is God cruel? Like the Old Testament, the New contains some texts that apparently exhibit a certain divine cruelty (e.g., Acts 5 where God kills two members of the Church because they cheated in respect of a real estate transaction). Is God violent and warlike? As we have seen, the Apocalypse of John repeats the Old Testament theme of a war against the wicked. Is God sanctimonious and are human beings mere sinners? It is the apostle Paul who presents humanity as suffering under the Law and as sinners from birth. Is God comprehensible? The New Testament, like the Old Testament, contains the idea of retribution (for example, Rom 2:5–6: the judgment of God that renders to each person according to his or her deeds) but also the vehement criticism of this notion in the passages where Jesus heals (for example, John 9) or in the Pauline affirmation of justification by faith.

Both Testaments insist on the freedom of an unknowable God[4] who "will be gracious to whom I will be gracious, and will show mercy on whom I will show mercy" (Exod 33:19 is taken up again in Rom 9:15). In any case, the idea of a definitive judgment as in Matthew 25 where the sinners

145

are eternally damned is lacking in the Old Testament, where each passage that deals with judgment leaves open the possibility of repentance—both God's and humankind's. Thus, the New Testament itself has its fair share of difficult texts that require unapologetic analysis.

It is important to remember that underlying both the Old Testament and the New Testament are confessions of faith: "God brought us out of Egypt" and "Christ died and was raised on the third day." The two confessions sum up the experience of a God of decisive freedom, from slavery and alienation, from death and sin. But the Hebrew Bible, like the New Testament, warns us against a triumphalist or self-centered exploitation of this confession by reminding us constantly that the God of the Bible should never be reduced to simply a "good God." Of course, Christians will always read the Hebrew Bible differently than the Jews, but Christians need to take seriously the fact that the Old Testament is more than a simple prologue. The God that the Hebrew Bible presents to Jews, to Christians, to the whole of humanity, has not finished questioning us, astonishing us, and calling into question our too-well-established theological ideas.

NOTES

Introduction

1. We refer to the religious syncretist Gnostic movement, which had its heyday in the second century AD. Gnosticism was characterized by dualism and by faith in redemption. Gnosis or "knowledge" allows man to find the essence of the divine in himself. The origins of Gnosticism are debatable: Is it a hellenization of Christianity, or does it have ancient Far Eastern influences, including Persian? And what links does it have with the dualist concepts of Judaism?

2. Johannes Salomon Semlerus, *Institutio ad doctrinam Christianam liberaliter discendam*, Halae Magdeburgicae, 1774, p. 79.

3. Adolf von Harnack, *Marcion. Das Evangelium vom fremden Gott*, 2nd ed. (Leipzig: J. C. Hinrichs, 1924), 217; English translation, *Marcion: The Gospel of the Alien God* (Eugene, OR: Wipf and Stock, 2007).

4. First edition, 1911; 10th ed., 1933.

5. Emmanuel Hirsch, *Das Alte Testament und die Predigt des Evangeliums* (Tübingen: J. C. B. Mohr, 1936).

6. Rudolf Bultmann, "Die Bedeutung des Alten Testaments fur den christlichen Glauben," in *Glauben und Verstehen* I, 7th ed. (Tübingen: J. C. B. Mohr, 1972), 313–36.

7. Interview with Jacques Pous in the Swiss journal *Le Courrier*, September 5, 2009. Jacques Pous is the author of *La tentation totalitaire: Essai sur les totalitarismes de la transcendance* (The Totalitarian Temptation: Essay on the Totalitarianism of Transcendence), (Paris: L'Harmattan, 2009).

8. We will return to this issue later. From now on, we will indicate the divine name by its four consonants: Yhwh.

9. The site of Qumran is near the Dead Sea. At Qumran, during the second and first centuries BC, there lived pious Jews who were in disagreement with the religious politics of Jerusalem. The archeological finds made there were among the most important

of the twentieth century. A great number of fragments of biblical books were found, but also writings intended especially for the community at Qumran.

10. From a historical perspective, it appears now that Israel was constituted as a federation of indigenous hill tribes that were in conflict with the Canaanite city-states.

11. For more detail see Thomas Römer, *The So-Called Deuteronomistic History: A Sociological, Historical and Literary Introduction* (London / New York: T & T Clark–Continuum, 2005).

12. For example, Ernst A. Knauf, *Ismael, Untersuchungen zur Geschichte Palästinas und Nordarabiens im I. Jahrtausend v. Chr.* ([ADPV]; Wiesbaden: Harrassowitz, 1985).

13. Scholars agree that the Pentateuch was composed by compiling and reworking different older documents or "sources." Whereas there is no more consensus on the existence or date of some of these sources, the distinction of "priestly texts" is widely acknowledged. These priestly texts were written in the sixth century BC by a group of priests either in Babylonia or in Jerusalem in order to promote the necessity of a sacrificial cult, but also to show that all the main rituals were already given since the very beginnings of the world and of Israel.

Chapter One

1. This is taken from Erhard S. Gertenberger, *Jahve—ein patriarchaler Gott?* (Stuttgart: Kohlhammer, 1988), 7.

2. During the royal period, the idea of creation often referred exclusively to the country in which the people of Israel lived. Other peoples are located "outside" and represent the forces of chaos against which the national god must fight.

3. The phrase "speak to her tenderly" expresses great intimacy. It is, perhaps, a euphemism for sexual relations.

4. In antiquity, the dream was common practice for entering into contact with a deity. One visits a sanctuary where one is "prepared" by the priests (sacrifices, drugs, etc.) for the encounter with the divine.

5. This expression is current in the Old Testament: Gen 14:10; Judges 17:2; 1 Sam 15:13; etc.

6. Judith Hadley, "Yahweh and 'His Ashera': Archaeological and

Textual Evidence for the Cult of the Goddess," in W. Dietrich and M. A. Klopfenstein, ed., *Ein Gott allein? JWHW—Verehrung und biblischer Monotheismus im Kontext der israelitischen und altorientalischen Religionsgeschichte,* ([OBO139] Fribourg/Göttingen: Vandenhoeck & Ruprecht, 1994): 235–68.

7. Nadav Na'aman and Nuri Lissovsky, "Kuntillet 'Ajrud, Sacred Trees and the Asherah," *Tel Aviv* 35 (2008): 186–208.

8. Klaus Koch, "Aschera als Himmelskönigin in Jerusalem," *Ugarit Forschungen* 20 (1988): 97–120.

9. Jacques Briend, *Dieu dans l'Ecriture* (God in Scripture), ([Lectio Divina 150] Paris: Cerf, 1992), 74; cf. also for the rest.

10. Cf. again 44:2, 24; 45:10; 66:13; etc.

Chapter Two

1. Immanuel Kant, *Der Streit der Fakultäten,* H. D. Brandt, P. Giordanti, ed. (Hamburg: Felix Meiner Verlag, 2005); English transl., Mary J. Gregor, *The Conflict of the Faculties* (New York: Abaris Books, 1979).

2. See *The Big Book of Jewish Humor,* edited and annotated by William Novak and Moshe Waldoks (New York: Harper & Row, 1981), 220. This joke is a classic and can also be found all over the Web.

3. Quoted from Abraham Segal, *Abraham: Enquête sur un Patriarche* (Abraham: Investigation of a Patriarch), (Paris: Plon, 1995), 412; new edition (Paris: Bayard, 2003).

4. Odil H. Steck, "Ist Gott grausam?" ("Is God cruel?"), in Wolfgang Bohme, ed., *Ist Gott grausam?* (Stuttgart: Evangelisches Verlagswerk, 1977).

5. Marie Balmary, *Le sacrifice interdit: Freud et la Bible* (The Forbidden Sacrifice: Freud and the Bible), (Paris: Grasset, 1987), 197; new edition (Biblio essais, 1995).

6. This is probably due to the fact that M. Balmary excludes any historical dimension when interpreting biblical texts; cf. the pertinent comments of Dominique Stein (also a psychoanalyst), *Lectures psychanalytiques de la Bible: l'enfant prodigue, Marie, saint Paul et les femmes* (Psychoanalytical Interpretations of the Bible), (Paris: Cerf, 1985).

7. The Hebrew expression literally means "go for you." It is an emphatic order.

8. On this subject, cf. the excellent article by Albert de Pury, "Le Dieu qui vient en adversaire. De quelques différences à propos de la perception de Dieu dans l'Ancien Testament" ("The God Who Comes as Adversary: Some Differences in the Perception of the God of the Old Testament"), in Raymond Kuntzmann, ed., *Ce Dieu qui vient: Mélanges offerts à Bernard Renaud* (The God Who Comes: Collected Essays in Honor of Bernard Renaud) ([Lectio Divina 159] Paris: Cerf, 1995), 45–67.

9. This is a euphemism for the genitals.

10. The root of this word denotes a kinsman by marriage (e.g., spouse, son-in-law, father-in-law). In Arabic, the same verb means "to circumcise."

11. Without doubt, that is what is behind Genesis 32. Compare Jacob's retrospective comment: "I have seen God face to face, and yet my life is preserved."

12. What is not clear is the true meaning of the name Israel, either "God reigns," *or* "God fights."

13. Andre Lacocque, *Le devenir de Dieu* (The Future of God), (Paris: Ed. Universitaires, 1967), 151.

Chapter Three

1. This approach is still practiced; cf. Giuseppe Barbaglio, *Dieu est-il violent? Une lecture des Ecritures juives et chretiennes* (Is God Violent? An interpretation of the Jewish and Christian scriptures), (Paris: Seuil, 1994).

2. The deportees were used in a number of ways. Some of them participated in the urbanization of Assyria (e.g., the construction of the city of Dur Sharrukin), others were employed at the Assyrian court, and still others were resold as slaves.

3. Cf. on this subject Norbert Lohfink, "Culture Shock and Theology: A Discussion of Theology as a Cultural and Sociological Phenomenon Based on the Example of Deuteronomic Law," *Biblical Theology Bulletin* 7 (1977): 12–22.

4. It is not entirely definite that the demographic explosion in Jerusalem is directly linked to the arrival of refugees from the old Kingdom of Israel, a view that M. Broshi especially defends in

"The Population of Ancient Jerusalem," *Revue Biblique* 92 (1975): 5–14; cf. the critical comments of Jean-Daniel Macchi, *Les Samaritains: Histoire d'une legende* (The Samaritans: A history of a legend), (Geneva: Labor et Fides [MdB 30], 1994), 129–31.

5. These treaties are available in English: translation: Simo Parpola and Kazuko Watanabe, *Neo-Assyrian Treaties and Loyalty Oaths*, SAA II (Helsinki: University Press, 1988).

6. I. Finkelstein and N. A. Silberman, *The Bible Unearthed: Archaeology's New Vision of Ancient Israel and the Origin of Its Sacred Texts* (New York: The Free Press, 1992).

7. Generally, this idea was part of the concept of a national god from whom the people expected interventions in order to protect his people in times of war. So in a well-known stele (ninth century BC), King Mesha of Moab thanks Kemosh, the tutelary god of Moab, for giving him victory over Israel.

8. Simo Parpola, *Assyrian Prophecies*, SAA IX (Helsinki: University Press, 1997), 4–5.

9. For more detail, cf. K. Lawson Younger, Jr., *Ancient Conquest Accounts: A Study in Ancient Near Eastern and Biblical History Writing* (Journal for the Study of the Old Testament, Supplement Series 98), (Sheffield, UK: JSOT Press, 1990), 61–124.

10. The text referred to is King Sargon's "Letter to God" II. Cf. Younger, 210–11 and 366–67.

11. Sara Japhet, "Postexilic Historiography: How and Why?" in *Israel Constructs Its History: Deuteronomistic Historiography in Recent Research*, ed. Albert de Pury, Thomas Römer, and Jean-Daniel Macchi, JSOT Sup 306 (Sheffield, UK: Sheffield Academic Press, 2000), 144–73.

12. Julius Wellhausen, *Prolegomena to the History of Ancient Israel* (Cleveland: Meridian Books, 1961), 182.

13. Deuteronomy 7:2 stipulates: "You must utterly destroy them." This is an allusion to a military practice whereby both the material booty and human booty are sacrificed to the deity so that the conquerors do not enrich themselves by their military victory.

14. Deuteronomy 7:3 says: "Do not intermarry with them, giving your daughters to their sons or taking their daughters for your sons"; Ezra 9:12 says: "Therefore do not give your daughters to their sons, neither take their daughters for your sons."

15. Only one text, Genesis 14, speaks of Abraham's involvement in a war. But everyone agrees that this text is in no way typ-

ical of the patriarchal tradition and that it is a later addition to the Abraham narrative.

Chapter Four

1. The *Epic of Gilgamesh* is a great classic of the ancient Near East, whose importance is similar to that of the Homeric epics in Greece, and which deals with many themes that are to be found in the Hebrew Bible: the flood, death, reflections on man's destiny, etc. See Maureen Gallery Kovacs, *The Epic of Gilgamesh* (Palo Alto, CA: Stanford University Press, 1989).

2. See the comments by Christophe Nihan, *From Priestly Torah to Pentateuch: A Study in the Composition of the Book of Leviticus*, FAT II/25 (Tübingen: Mohr Siebeck), 2007), 598–607.

3. In the Old Testament, as elsewhere in the ancient Near East, homosexual relations between two men (well evidenced) are a problem because of the inequality of the sexes. In a homosexual exchange, a man seems to play the role of the woman, and that is considered shameful. In fact, the Old Testament does not recognize stable homosexual relationships, such as are recognized in Western societies. For more details, see Thomas Römer and Loyse Bonjour, *L'homosexualité dans le Proche-Orient ancien et la Bible* (Homosexuality in the ancient Near East and the Bible), Essais bibliques 37 (Geneva: Labor et Fides), 2005.

Chapter Five

1. Roger Dadoun, *La violence: Essai sur l' "homo violens"* (Violence: an essay on "homo violens"), Optique 203. Philosophie (Paris: Hatier, 1993), 9.

2. Some lines of enquiry are developed in *Le Monde de la Bible* (The World of the Bible), 105, 1997, on the story of Cain and Abel.

3. The difficulty of verse 7 comes principally from the fact that the word *sin* is in the feminine while the verb forms are masculine.

4. See the beginning of chapter 4 on the fall of Adam and Eve.

5. In fact, these were canals and not rivers.

6. This updated version is taken from Walter Dietrich and Christian Link, *Die dunklen Seiten Gottes: Willkür und Gewalt*, vol.

1 (God's Dark Sides: Despotism and Violence), (Neukirchen-Vluyn: Neukirchener, 1995), 209–10.

7. Similarly, we can mention the adaptation of the psalms of vengeance by the Latin American theologian Ernesto Cardenal, *The Psalms of Struggle and Liberation* (St. Louis: Herder and Herder, 1971).

Chapter Six

1. For more detail on this tradition, cf. Thomas Römer, *Les chemins de la sagesse: Proverbes, Job, Ecclesiastes* (The Ways of Wisdom: Proverbs, Job, Ecclesiastes), (Poliez-le-Grand: Editions du Moulin, 1999).

2. In John 9. However, Jesus then contests the disciples' logic, saying, "Neither this man nor his parents sinned; he was born blind so that God's works might be revealed in him" (v 3).

3. Rene Girard, *La route antique des hommes pervers* (The ancient road of evil men), (Paris: Grasset, 1985).

4. Robert A. Heinlein, *Job: A Comedy of Justice* (New York: Del Rey/Ballantine Books, 1985). In this satirical novel, a devout man traverses parallel worlds, the victim of a superior and apparently arbitrary power.

5. See Ernst A. Knauf, "La patrie de Job" (Job's homeland), in Samuel Terrien, *Job*, 2nd ed. updated (Geneva: Labor et Fides [CAT 13], 2005), 12–27.

6. Othmar Keel, *Jahwes Entgegnung an Job: Eine Deutung von Job 38–41 vor dem Hintergrund der zeitgenössischen Bildkunst* (Job responds to God. An interpretation of Job 38–41 on the background of ancient iconography), (Göttingen: Vandenhoeck & Ruprecht [FRLANT 121], 1978).

7. See, for example, the (good) translation in the *Nouvelle Bible Segond*: "This is why I give up: I repent in dust and ashes."

8. In modern Hebrew, *hebel*, in fact, means "absurdity." For a philosophical approach to Ecclesiastes, see also Alain Bühlmann, *La structure logique du livre de Ecclesiastes ou comment être sage sous les Ptolémées?* (The logical structure of the book of Ecclesiastes or how to be wise under the Ptolemies), (Munich: Gorg [BN Beihefte 12], 2000).

9. Genesis 9 emphasizes the conflicted aspect of interhuman

relations, but also human beings' relationship with the animals. Contrary to Genesis 1 where human beings as well as animals are created vegetarian, after the flood the animals can serve to nourish mankind through the institution of the sacrifice, which acts here as a way of managing violence and establishing communication between God and mankind.

10. John Chrysostom, *On the Incomprehensibility of Divine Nature*, trans. Paul W. Harkins (Washington, DC: Catholic University of America Press, 1984).

11. There remains, it is true, a certain ambiguity regarding the end of the book that is normally translated as a rhetorical question: "And should I not pity Nineveh?" (Jonah 4:11). In the Hebrew text, there is nothing to indicate that it should not be translated like this. It could also be understood as "I will not pity Nineveh," which goes against the sense of the text. But the ambiguity is perhaps deliberate because the reader knows that Nineveh was completely destroyed by the Babylonians. So the text plays with the relationship between God's judgment and freedom. In any case, Jonah presents a God who is not constrained by narrow doctrine.

Conclusion

1. Wilhelm Vischer, *Das Christuszeugnis des Alten Testaments* (The Witness of the Old Testament to Christ), vol. 1 (Zollikon/Zürich: Evangelischer Verlag, 1934).

2. Remember that the Hebrew Bible as we know it—that is, divided into three parts (Law, Prophets, Writings)—did not exist before the second century AD.

3. Compare, for example, the story of the killing of newborn boys ordered by the enemy king in both Exodus 1–2 and Matthew 2; or again, Jesus' Sermon on the Mount in Matthew 5–7, which several times recalls the communication of the Law by Moses on Mount Sinai.

4. The question in Romans 9:20—"But who indeed are you, a human being, to argue with God?"—harks back to God's response to Job.